COMING

OF AGE IN

BUFFALO

COMING

OF AGE IN

BUFFALO

Youth and Authority in the Postwar Era

WILLIAM GRAEBNER

Temple University Press   Philadelphia

Temple University Press,
Philadelphia 19122
Copyright © 1990 by Temple University.
All rights reserved
Published 1990
Printed in the United States of America

Library of Congress Cataloging-in-Publication Data

Graebner, William.
    Coming of age in Buffalo : youth and authority
in the postwar era / William Graebner.
        p.   cm.
    Includes index.
    ISBN 13: 978-1-56639-197-9 (paper : alk. paper)
    1. Youth—New York (State)—Buffalo—
History—20th century.
    2. Buffalo (N.Y.)—Social conditions.   I. Title.
HQ796.G6995   1989
305.2′35′0974797—dc 19   88-27283
                                          CIP

080612P

For Michael Higgins and

the people of Buffalo

CONTENTS

vii

P R E F A C E

My work on the history of Buffalo youth began about five years ago as a traditional scholarly undertaking, inspired by an abiding interest in systems and relationships of authority, by a growing attachment to the city of Buffalo and, as my teenage son suspects, by a reluctance to give up the ghost of my youth.

The project took a different direction in 1985, when Rollie Adams, then Director of the Buffalo and Erie County Historical Society, encouraged me to move toward a major public exhibit of photographs and artifacts. With a grant from the New York State Council on the Arts, the exhibit opened in September 1986. It ran for a year (in fact, portions of it still circulate at local banks and shopping malls) and proved to be the single most important experience of my professional life. For the first time, my work—me, my ideas, my ways of seeing and organizing the world—became accessible to my friends and to the community.

I am grateful to Rollie, for his vision and confidence, and to the Buffalo and Erie County Historical Society; to Thomas Payne, for dogged and decisive assistance in organizing materials for public consumption; to Michael Higgins, for printing the exhibit photographs; to Mary Simmons-Smillie, for producing over 700 8 × 10 inch prints, some of which appear in this book; and to Joan Tondra of Tondra & Stern, for a brilliant catalogue design that captured not only the exhibit but the spirit of the postwar era. I am also indebted to those who talked with me about their lives as teenagers in Buffalo, and whose recollections and photographs make this book possible. Special thanks go to Dave Schnell, Lee Johansson, Jerry Szefel, Al Triem, David Holdsworth, Bob Prince, Cliff Pritchard, Patricia Guarino, Joe Greco, Ernie Corallo, Tom Scherer, Bob DeSoto, Margaret Russ, June Bihl, Daniel Majchrzak, Betty Lou Eisenmann, Dan Petrelli, Rose Gallivan, Danny Chudoba, B. John Tutuska, Rose Ann Bruno, Bob Sniatecki, Tony

Sperry, James Pickens, Robert Rush, Michael and Marjorie Tritto, Steve Gross, Danny McBride, Bernie Sandler, Van Miller, Ralph Powers, Joseph Manch, Sheila Malone, Burton Glaser, Gretchen Martin, Carol Sue Roll, Angelo and Ange Coniglio, Gail Whitman, Virginia Kelley, Jim Lee, Dorothy Gallagher, Dick Hirsch, Robert Depczynski, Bill Robinson, Zaid Islam, Tommy Owen, Bob Menz, Frank Lorenz, Ed Gralnik, Thelma Hardiman, Juanita Melford, Mary Carter, Ruth Richardson, Johnnie Mayo, Paul Missana, John Wojtowicz, Bob Wells, Albert and Walter Marquart and Broadway Knitting Mills, Robert Bryce, Mike Sendlbeck, Spain Rodriguez, and Frank Palombaro.

This book is an effort to merge different approaches to the past, to blend traditional scholarship and public history. I have tried to keep the book appealing and relevant for general and local readers—the kinds of people who shared their scrapbooks and photographs, and who appear on the pages that follow—and yet to make the book useful for the academic historian. If I have reached an appropriate balance, credit is due my editor Janet Francendese, whose enthusiasm, trust, and persistence buoyed my spirits through several revisions. I also wish to thank anonymous readers for Temple University Press, *American Studies*, the *Journal of American History*, and *Radical History Review*; Dianne Bennett, who read various drafts with a critical eye to language, organization, and content; Jay Heffron, who assisted with some of the research; Mia Boynton, who interviewed several persons; and George Lipsitz, for his wonderfully rich and insightful review of the manuscript. The State University of New York at Fredonia made possible a leave of absence and provided financial aid for a portion of the oral history interviews. Early research was supported by a grant-in-aid from the American Association for State and Local History.

Buffalo, New York
December 7, 1988

COMING OF AGE IN BUFFALO

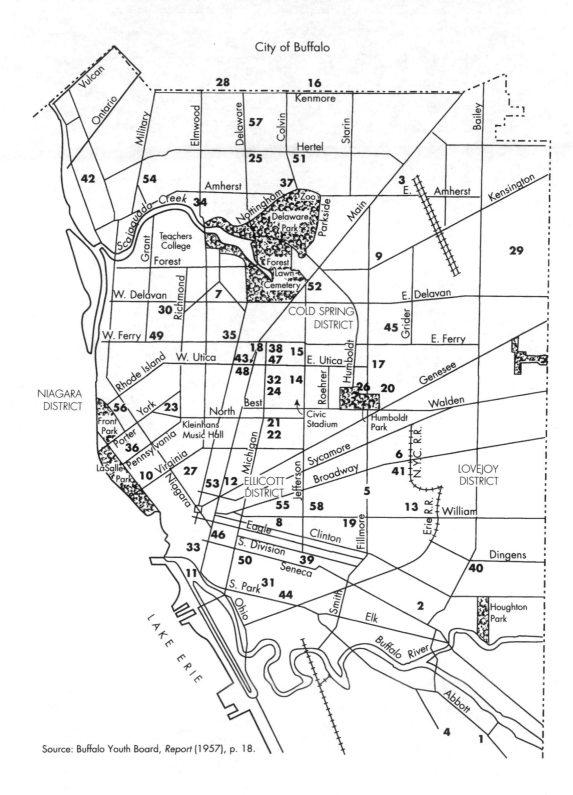

City of Buffalo

Source: Buffalo Youth Board, *Report* (1957), p. 18.

KEY TO MAP

1. Abbott Rd. and Meriden St.
2. Babcock Boys Club
3. Bennett High School
4. Bishop Timon High School
5. Black Ts
6. Broadway Knitting Mills
7. Buffalo Seminary
8. Buffalo Technical High School
9. Burgard Vocational High School
10. Butler-Mitchell Boys Club (1943 location)
11. Canadiana Dock
12. Center Theater
13. Central Terminal
14. Civic Stadium
15. Cold Spring District
16. Colvin Theater
17. Deco Restaurant
18. Delwood Ballroom
19. Dold's Playground
20. East High School
21. Fosdick-Masten Park High School
22. Fruit Belt
23. Grover Cleveland High School
24. Gunners (Masten/Dodge)
25. Holy Spirit
26. Humboldt Park/Park Gang
27. Hutchinson-Central High School
28. Kenmore
29. Kensington High School
30. Lafayette High School
31. Louisiana and South Park (corner lounging)
32. Masten/Southampton
33. Memorial Auditorium
34. McKinley Vocational High School
35. Nardin Academy
36. Niagara Police Station
37. Nichols School
38. Offerman Stadium
39. Public School No. 6
40. Peruvians
41. Regal Restaurant
42. Riverside High School
43. Royal Arms
44. Sam the wailin' tailor
45. Seneca Vocational High School
46. Shelton Square
47. Shrine Teen Canteen
48. Skateland
49. Ray Spasiano's tailor shop
50. St. Lucy's
51. St. Margaret's
52. St. Vincent's
53. Statler Hotel
54. Tropical Inn
55. Willert Projects
56. Working Boys Home
57. YMCA Delaware Branch
58. Zanzibar Lounge

atter

Y. Finds

n Shock Force Effective

n summons for
e owner $15. An
e is levied if the
a car pound, and
reclaimed, $1 a
charged. After

30 days, Mr. Mulrain may sell the car at auction. On June 23, nearly 100 cars were auctioned in the Bronx.

The Sanitation Department says there has been a big improvement since alternate-side parking was begun. Buffalo's alternate parking plan, officials say, is stymied because there is no money for signs.

New York is not bragging too much yet, but Mr. Mulrain says residents and visitors have sent communications noting a marked improvement in cleanliness in New York City.

DISC JOCKEY ATOP SIGN CAUSES JAM IN SHELTON SQUARE

The antics of a disc jockey atop a sign about 75 feet above Shelton Square Sunday afternoon caused an ear-shattering traffic jam, brought out a fire aerial-ladder truck and four police cars and landed the WWOL employe in jail.

Thomas Clague, 25, of 91 16th St., who broadcasts as Guy King, was charged with disorderly conduct after Commissioner DeCillis determined the station had no permit for the demonstration. Police also served Clague with a warrant dated Jan. 7 which charges Clague ignored a parking tag.

He spent more than six hours in the cellblock in Police Headquarters until Assistant Detective Chief Leo V. Swanekamp ordered him released in the custody of City Judge Michael E. Zimmer. King was served with the traffic warrant while in the cell. Police today said Clague will be arraigned tomorrow in City Court.

It was the second time Clague had jammed traffic in S Square and caused an ea ting din with his radioed i tions to motorists to honk horns. On May 8 police a his demonstration to co after Commissioner DeCill proved it.

The aerial ladder truck w patched from Hook & Lad when a caller telephoned that a man was trapped o roof. Clague, however, ma own way back to the st studios. The four police were necessary to untang traffic jam.

554 Main Street
own Buffalo, phone CL. 5060

ESTABLISHED 1832

BARGAIN JUBILEE

SHOP
TONIGHT
'TIL 9

T H E M E S

It was July 3, 1955, and high above Buffalo's Shelton Square a special kind of independence was being declared. Wearing bermuda shorts, WWOL disc jockey Guy King had climbed out a studio window, microphone in hand, to broadcast from atop a large billboard. King called on motorists caught in the traffic jam below—many of them teenagers who had jumped in their cars and come downtown just to be part of the event—to honk their horns if they wanted to hear the song he was playing. Honk they did, as King held forth to the repeated strains of Bill Haley and the Comets and "Rock Around the Clock."[1]

The independence that King proclaimed that day was, in part, the independence of the young, an independence contested less in physical combat (though the uproar over juvenile delinquency suggests that there was some of that, too) than in a series of struggles over music, dance, clothing, language, style, the automobile, and other facets of what future sociologists would call "youth culture."

For all its simplicity, the Shelton Square incident contained several important ingredients of the new youth culture. Unlike the 1776 Declaration, this one was not written but broadcast, and its artifact was not a document but a 45 rpm record. Records, radio, disc jockeys, concert promoters, comic books, movies, and movie stars—the media and media personalities were central to the emerging youth culture (so much so, in fact, that disc jockeys like King would be held responsible for rock 'n' roll and other supposed adolescent excesses). The centerpiece of the event, Haley's "Rock Around the Clock," proclaimed a freedom from the constraints of time that was all the more meaningful for being entirely mythical; and "rock," a word taken from black culture, at once suggested the liberating possibilities of dancing and sex. The song itself, its place heightened by its use in the film *Blackboard Jungle*, gave notice that this new generation would invent

5

rather than inherit the music that would play such a significant part in generational politics. And the larger event in Shelton Square—the "demonstration," as the police labeled it—was a product of the mobility, demographic power, and affluence (they had to have horns to honk) of the nation's first generation of "teenagers."

Yet this view of the Shelton Square incident as a symbolic episode in a great generational rebellion, launched by teens against the adult and parental standard bearers of an earlier age, presents an incomplete and somewhat distorted picture of the youth culture of the postwar era. There were, in fact, *many* Buffalo youth cultures, differentiated by social class, neighborhood, race, ethnicity, education, religion, and gender—and not all of them were represented by Guy King and Bill Haley. Buffalo's working-class teenagers were more likely to tune in to George "Hound Dog" Lorenz, whose live evening broadcasts over WKBW featured rhythm and blues, the music of the blacks, lustier than anything Haley recorded. Many of the city's middle-class, white teenage girls, put off by the Hound's music and brusque demeanor, could be found at the Delwood Ballroom on Main Street at Utica, where on Saturday afternoons the genial and paternal Bob Wells held forth with his popular "Hi-Teen" program. Similarly, one's place in the social structure determined whether one wore khakis or levis, sported a DA or a brush cut, joined a high school fraternity or a street gang, volunteered for the March of Dimes or committed acts of "juvenile delinquency." So fragmented was the culture of youth that by 1956 and 1957, black and white teenagers were fighting in the streets, in downtown movie houses, at the Crystal Beach amusement park and on the Crystal Beach boat, the *Canadiana*, and in other public spaces. Although most Buffalo youth would have applauded the sentiments expressed in "Rock Around the Clock," they would have understood that title in very different ways.

This reading of Haley's song and of the Guy King episode suggests a central theme of the following pages: that the history of youth can best be constructed not as the history of a single culture—though one cannot deny the existence of some sort of youth culture—but as the story of disparate subcultures, united by age but in conflict over class, race, ethnicity, and gender. Consistent with this emphasis, I will also argue that idea of a youth culture was as much a social myth as a social reality, a representation of a culture of affluence and consensus that existed primarily in the collective imagination of the dominant culture.[2]

A second theme—an approach, really—cuts against the tendency of the subcultural method to locate youth within particularistic categories. Though Buffalo teenagers engaged social reality largely through those categories—as middle class or working class, as blacks or whites, as participants or nonparticipants in media-based youth activities—they were also bound by certain universal stories, stories that circulated beyond the subcultures that lived them. Something of a general Buffalo "youth culture" may be found in these stories: in Guy King's antics, in the broadcasts of "Hound Dog" Lorenz, in Bob Wells's Hi-Teen Club, in the public school Dress Right code, in the 1953 rumble between the Park Gang and the Gunners, and in the *Canadiana* riot of 1956.

A third theme is the all-encompassing program of social engineering that made the fantasy of independence expressed in Haley's song and King's confrontational billboard broadcasting so vital to postwar teenagers. Made anxious and fearful by rock 'n' roll, juvenile delinquency, pegged pants, and other phenomena that were understood as part of a new, antiauthoritarian teenage lifestyle, parents and other adult authorities in the Buffalo area imposed a bewildering variety of controls and sanctions. Municipal and state agencies sought to replace teenagers' unstructured and unsupervised leisure with teen centers and other forms of supervised "recreation." The Catholic Church maintained an active youth program under the Catholic Youth Organization (CYO), served as area censor of popular culture, and tolerated Monsignor Franklin Kelliher's old-fashioned methods for dealing with juvenile delinquents, practiced at his Working Boys Home on Vermont Street. King's example to the contrary, Buffalo's print and radio media resisted the more radical tendencies in the new youth culture. Programs such as Wells's "Hi-Teen" and Bernie Sandler's "Young Crowd" were designed to insulate their relatively conservative, middle-class audiences from the music and dress of delinquent, working-class, and black subcultures and to encourage listeners to appreciate more traditional musical forms handed down by adults.

Because postwar youths spent so much of their time in the high schools, these institutions were the locus of the most consistent efforts to shape their behavior and values. Virtually every school institution and program, from the prom to the lunchroom, from graduation to the student council, was called upon to assist in creating a more responsible student population. High school fraternities and sororities, deemed inimical to the goal of school unity and loyalty, were discouraged. The most influential of Buffalo's school programs was Dress

Right, a voluntary dress code authored by students under administration aegis and packaged for national consumption as the Buffalo Plan.

Whether private or public, these efforts at social engineering shared a dual and, at first glance, paradoxical perspective. On the one hand, the rhetoric and actions of Buffalo's social engineers seemed to suggest the desire for a more unified and homogeneous society—a "democratic" society built on "toleration." Youth culture proferred an age-graded society, and its centrifugal tendencies threatened the high school's role as an institution of democratic assimilation and homogenization. To create an atmosphere of unity and agreement, educators, church leaders, judges, radio personalities, and others interested in the behavior of youth employed a democratic, participatory methodology adapted from progressive education. Similarly, the injunction to strive for "maturity," so common in the late 1940s and early 1950s, seemed to summon *all* teenagers to eschew the chimeras of youth.

On the other hand, the limits of unity and homogeneity were never far from the surface. The reformers' agenda did not encompass programs that might have chipped away at barriers of race and class, and the authority of adults was in no important way challenged by the limited participation granted youth. Even the call to maturity was issued differentially to working-class and middle-class youth. In a curious way, then, the proponents of social unity were also engaged, actively and consciously, in perpetuating social divisions.

This ubiquitous and passionate adult intervention also poses problems for the study of youth culture. Because virtually every aspect of youth culture was penetrated by adults, "pure" expressions of youth culture occur infrequently. Certainly graduation addresses, school yearbooks, and student newspapers must be considered impure sources, mediated by adult ideas and values, and the daily newspapers, as valuable as they are, covered youth from an adult perspective—that is, only insofar as youth were found to be learning the skills of responsible citizenship, coming under appropriate supervision, or threatening the foundations of the social order. Although I used oral interviews as a way to compensate for the biases inherent in the printed sources, to a significant extent I have allowed the sources their due. As a result, this book is less about the lives of teenagers than it is about the interface of youth culture and subcultures with the dominant, middle-class culture of the adult world.

Even within this framework, my approach and inclinations are at odds with recent tendencies in the reading and interpretation of culture. The current perspective sees culture as relatively open and fluid, a field of opportunity, according to anthropologist Edward M. Bruner, in which people are "active agents in the historical process" and the impulse for change is not exogenous to the social system but intrinsic to it. "Selves, social organizations, and cultures," writes Bruner, "are not given but are problematic and always in production. Cultural change, cultural continuity, and cultural tranmission all occur simultaneously in the experiences and expressions of social life."[3]

Although most scholars acknowledge the existence of a "dominant culture" dedicated to perpetuating its dominance through some kind of hegemonic apparatus, they also allow for considerable play in this process. The dominant culture is held to be something less than monolithic, beset by differences and divisions that create the opportunity for alternative ideas and practices. Similarly, as Raymond Williams has written, hegemonic structures must be "continually . . . renewed, recreated and defended," thus making change not only possible but, in a certain sense, a natural byproduct of the effort to maintain cultural dominance.[4]

Others examine culture "from the bottom up," emphasizing the extent to which subordinated cultures and subcultures are able to oppose and resist the hegemony of the dominant culture, or to negotiate "space" from it.[5] John Clarke's approach to style develops Levi-Strauss's concept of *bricolage*, according to which the objects offered by the dominant culture are transformed and recontextualized by subcultures in a pattern that "carries a new meaning"; Erica Carter attempts to demonstrate how a girl's purchase of Perlon stockings, while ostensibly a function of the incorporation of youth into a commodity culture, in fact represents an act of willful "self-determination." While acknowledging the "pervasive" and determinative effect of ideology, Janice Radway argues that ideology "does not preclude the possibility of firm though limited resistance," in this case the resistance of women engaged in the process of reading romance novels. Such resistance is possible because "interstices still exist within the social fabric." Though "minimal" and incapable of altering a "woman's situation," resistance is to be studied because otherwise "we have already conceded the fight."[6]

The fight should not be conceded, but neither can it be won by trumpeting minor victories, searching for "interstices" where resistance might take place, and presenting culture as if it were infinitely malleable by ordinary people. This has been the dominant strategy of the Left for too long. What is needed is a more realistic appreciation of the limited opportunities available for opposition, resistance, and change, as well as better understanding of the tools available to the dominant culture. Only then can we begin to think about dismantling a system that allows little scope for human intervention, tolerates change only on the margins, and permits only minor victories.

CULTURE AND SUBCULTURE

TYPICAL TEENS

n 1957, the U.S. Information Agency (USIA) added to its archive another portrait of a "typical American teenager." This one featured Brennan Jacques, playing piano in his own orchestra, the "Fabulous Esquires." The problem, of course, was that Jacques's apparel, avocation, and admiring peer group identified him as "typical" only of a particular subculture: white, upwardly mobile, upper middle class.

The USIA's error was understandable enough; after all, the agency had a country to market, and the term "typical teenager" effectively masked differences in race, ethnicity, and class. But we must be wary of making the same mistake today in looking back on Buffalo's youth culture. The term "youth culture" may be the academic equivalent of "typical teenager"; like its predecessor, it implies that there was one unified culture in which all youth participated and through which all youth expressed similar values. And that is a bit like suggesting that the peoples of the world share a basic humanity—true enough, but not a very useful proposition.

Contrary to the mythic past created by memory and shaped by the media, youth culture was not an invention of the post–World War II era. As early as the 1830s, urbanization and industrialization were beginning to undermine farm and craft economies and to produce dependent and school-based adolescents. Pre–Civil War youth came together in "gangs," committed acts of "juvenile delinquency," and created a street-based youth culture that would trouble 1950s adults. High school fraternities and sororities, though deemed more socially responsible than gangs, were considered troublesome enough to be prohibited by a number of states in the Progressive Era. High school enrollments, one sign of the separa-

Original caption: "Washington, D.C. —Brennan Jacques, a typical American teenager, has his own orchestra, the 'Fabulous Esquires,' composed of youngsters aware of what their schoolmates like and do not like in current music. Here, young Jacques plays the piano for a group of young people who have gathered around him." 1957. United States Information Agency, National Archives.

tion from family and workplace that marked the emergence of a culture of youth, steadily increased beginning in the 1920s, when growing numbers of college-bound young adults created a functional peer-group culture that helped them learn to compete, to cooperate, and to consume in a modern capitalist economy. Theories of delinquency—theories that at once described and embellished the new reality of functionless dependence—achieved prominence in 1904 with the publication of G. Stanley Hall's *Adolescence*. A few years later, Jane Addams found the "modern city" responsible for separating "the pleasures of the young and mature." And the American social service agencies that emerged to regulate and contain this new culture of youth were by and large Progressive-era products.[7]

Nonetheless, the term "youth culture" has a certain utility. It can help us appreciate the ways in which history, rather than subculture, shaped the lives of youth—how, for example, the experience of youth in the 1940s and 1950s was different from that of Depression-era youth or from the generation that came of age during the Vietnam and civil rights protests of the late 1960s. The term can also help us cut across subcultures to reveal the most significant ways—including music, clothing, and leisure activities—in which youth of all subcultures expressed, defined, and organized themselves at a particular historical moment.

COMING OF AGE IN BUFFALO

Certain characteristics of the process of coming of age in the 1940s and 1950s—characteristics that have as much to do with World War II, the Cold War, and the quality of domestic existence in postwar America as they do with any peculiarities of life in the Queen City—determined the shape of postwar youth culture. Far from being the artificially drawn-out and hence alienating experience that many scholars have described, for many youths adolescence was a relatively brief process, hurried along by adults hoping to rush adolescents to "maturity." Adolescence was often abruptly terminated by graduation from high school, early marriage (the median age of first marriage fell rapidly throughout the 1940s and early 1950s, reaching a low of 20.1 years for women in 1956), and the beginning of a large, "baby boom" family.[8]

It was also a process increasingly identified not with the home or the neighborhood, but with high school. In 1920, the high schools educated less than a

Dorothy and Dave Gallagher lived the abstraction known as the baby boom. The first photograph shows the Gallaghers just two weeks after their marriage. Six years later, they literally had their hands full. Courtesy, Dorothy Gallagher.

third of the nation's population of fourteen- to seventeen-year-olds; by 1940, the figure had risen to 73 percent, and by 1960 to 87 percent.[9] As this happened, the schools became points of contact for youth populations that had heretofore been largely separate. Blacks went to school with whites, working class with middle class, those who wanted to be there with those who did not. Although the

S
C
H
O
O
L

P
O
L
L

1. Do you expect to finish college?

Yes - - - - -	87%
No - - - - -	13%

2. Do you approve of going steady?

Yes - - - - -	66%
No - - - - -	34%

3. In a boy what most attracts you?

Good looks - - - -	2%
Affluence - - - -	.6%
Social behavior - - -	4.4%
Appeal - - - -	23%
Personality - - - -	70%

4. Do you think there is going to be a war with Russia?

Within 1 year - - -	8%
Within 3 years - - -	36%
Within 5 years - - -	25%
Within 10 years - - -	11%
Never - - - -	20%

5. At what age do you expect to be married?

Never - - - -	2%
17 - 19 - - - -	7%
20 - 22 - - - -	61%
23 - 25 - - - -	29%
Later than 25 - - -	1%

Student opinion at an elite girls' school. Buffalo Seminary, *The Seminaria*, 1951.

schools rushed to homogenize these newly differentiated student bodies under the slogans of "democracy" and "loyalty," the commingling inevitably produced tension, conflict, and—even more disturbing for some adults—a certain middle-class admiration for, and emulation of, working-class and black subcultures.

World War II shaped the lives of Buffalo youth in many ways. Like other cities that were centers of war production, Buffalo was crowded, its more than 600,000 residents pressing against the limits of available land and resources. Certain sections of the city—the Niagara, Ellicott, and Lovejoy districts—were especially saturated, and these areas would experience high rates of youth arrests and juvenile delinquency in the immediate postwar years.[10] Many of the new migrants were blacks from the South, come to northern cities to participate in the wartime economy. As this black population grew and migrated into previously all-white neighborhoods, racial conflict became a feature of Buffalo's youth culture.

The war brought youth from the margins of a Depression-era economy into central roles as producers and consumers. Sixteen- and seventeen-year-olds, too young for military service, went to work at Curtiss-Wright and other area plants. Several hundred members of the Butler-Mitchell Boys Club signed up to spend the summer of 1943 harvesting for area farmers while living at a Fresh Air Mis-

Blacks and whites making contact in the high schools.

The first known photograph of "giving five." *Lafayette Oracle,* 1955.

Buffalo Technical, *Techtonian,* 1953.

A cartoonist's humorous treatment of racial tensions. Cartoon by Tredo, Buffalo Technical, *Techtonian,* 1957.

sion camp at Angola, and that fall, the opening of Buffalo's public schools was delayed almost a week so that children could continue to work on the farms. Those too young to work or to fight had nonetheless to shoulder a heavy burden of wartime responsibility to country and self. Thus the 1943 graduating class at Public School No. 6 was counseled by Superintendent Robert T. Bapst to recognize and "resolutely measure up to" the responsibilities that went with "one's position in life."[11]

As producers and consumers, Buffalo youths matured rapidly during the war, in the process acquiring qualities of self-reliance and independence that would

Off to work at the Victory Farm Cadet Camp, Angola, New York, 1945. Courtesy, Paul Missana and the Buffalo Boys Clubs.

soon clash with traditional adult notions of youth's proper place in the social order. The *Buffalo Criterion*, serving the city's black community, commented on the disturbing fact that many sixteen-year-old boys and girls were earning more money than their parents. One result of the "unequalled freedom that money brings," claimed the *Criterion*, was a new pattern of nighttime street life, characterized by "rowdies," "would-be toughies," and an increase in the number of "pickups." Youth, concluded the *Criterion* in 1944, "is catering to more wild parties and patterning closely behind many adults with whom they work side by side." [12]

Although the *Criterion* linked the wartime increase in antisocial behavior to affluence and association with adults, there is another theory that the postwar cult of male toughness may have been a product of the awkward contrast between the foxhole soldier, on the one hand, and the comfortable civilian on the other. In any event, the ideal of male toughness, captured in the late 1940s in Mickey Spillane's violence-prone private eye, Mike Hammer, remained strong into the 1950s, appearing in forms as distinct as Marlon Brando's image of rebellion in *The Wild One* (1954) and the high school mania for wrestling, football, and other combative sports. [13]

Perhaps the most important consequence of youth's wartime economic experi-

Riverside High School students celebrate the Allied victory—or anticipated victory—in World War II. Riverside *Skipper*, 1945.

"We were proud to have a boyfriend in uniform." C. 1954. Courtesy, Gail Whitman.

ence, however, came from the dramatic changes in status brought about by the end of the war in 1945. Although youths welcomed the cessation of conflict—to the point of sculpting a "V" in their hair to show it—many young people who had worked during the war resented returning to the artificial and statusless world of high school and found it difficult to give up their jobs to returning veterans. It was partly for this reason that postwar high schools experienced high dropout rates.[14]

The war and the atmosphere of international tension that hung over America throughout the 1940s and into the 1950s had a special set of meanings for adolescent girls. Even during World War II, relatively few girls went into the service. At Riverside High School, for example, a 1945 survey found 1,415 Riverside youth in the military, only 61 of them girls. Those who remained sold savings bonds, wrote to boys in the service, cultivated the art of dancing with other girls, and found themselves—even after the war—in classes that lacked a significant male presence. For some girls, the military uniform took on a powerful mystique. "I made up my mind," recalls one woman, "that I was going to go out with one from every branch of the service. We were proud to have a boyfriend in uniform."[15]

After 1945, Buffalo youth would experience an age of affluence and, with the exception of the Korean War, of peace. But it was an affluence that could be appreciated only against the backdrop of the Great Depression of the 1930s, and it was a peace haunted by the Cold War and the bomb. School yearbooks suggest that students in Buffalo high schools—at least the mainstream students who wrote for the yearbook and whose views most closely tracked those of administrators—understood the Cold War much as diplomat and scholar George Kennan described it in 1947: as an ideological struggle between two alien systems and ways of life.[16] On one side were war, dictatorship, "tyranny," and collectivism; on the other side—much more comprehensively described in the yearbooks— were peace, "freedom," individualism, and, above all, democracy. Because the Cold War was often conceptualized as an ideological struggle, the victor would naturally be the side that held most tightly to its ideals. Since the opponent was insidiously clever, it was especially vital that ignorant and therefore vulnerable Americans be educated to resist the enemy's "false philosophies" and "wiles." "A well-informed people," said the 1947 Lafayette High School salutatorian, "is the best defense a nation can have against demagogues that may rise and against those groups who wish to destroy our form of government."

As a result of this kind of thinking, Buffalo youth came of age in schools that were ideological training camps, where administrators labored to demonstrate the superiority of the "system" of democracy. This training took many different forms. As the Cold War deepened in 1949 and 1950, new student governments were created at Lafayette and at Bishop Timon, while at Seneca Vocational proceedings of the Student Court were described by the associate superintendent as "a truly fine example of democracy in action." Another sign of the impact of the Cold War on Buffalo high schools was the widespread interest in world affairs. Beginning in the late 1940s, students flocked to such organizations as the World Affairs Club at Riverside and the Junior Council on World Affairs at Buffalo Technical. A national high school poster contest on the theme "Meat and the Nation's Welfare" brought forth one effort titled "Eat Meat/To Keep Our Nation Strong" and another labeled "Meat/America's Power, Europe's Prayer." Throughout the postwar era, student leaders and administrators urged students to reject complacency and accept the responsibilities of world leadership.

The Cold War was more than just a matter of foreign policy, more even than an ideological field of force requiring youths to mouth democratic pieties. The logic of the Cold War, as historian Robert Wiebe has written, "drew a line

Keeping the nation strong meant eating meat, to be sure. But according to this student poster, it also meant a sharp division of labor in which women were relegated to child-rearing roles. Bennett Beacon, commencement issue, 1948.

between friends and enemies," exhorting Americans "to perfect their internal homogeneity." [17] As long as this logic held sway, deviation from generally accepted cultural norms, whether in hair style, music, clothes, or conduct, would be understood by adults and school administrators—and even some students—as socially irresponsible. Thus the postwar thrust toward conformity and homogeneity, so frequently mentioned as a factor in postwar culture, was in some sense a function of the Cold War. And features of the cultural landscape as trivial as the injunction to be loyal to one's school or as minor as the crewcut—a haircut characterized by uniformity—can be understood as part of the culture of the Cold War.

This generation was the first to come of age with the bomb. In Buffalo, at least, this formidable task was accomplished with stolid acceptance, seriousness of purpose, and, in more than one case, with wit and humor. It was 1947 when Riverside High School students learned in assembly about the technical operation of the atomic bomb. After 1950, students lined the halls in air raid drills, learned where the crackers were stored in local fallout shelters, or made light of civil defense procedures. The 1957 launching of the Russian satellite Sputnik found Riverside students ready to meet the Soviet challenge with their own weapon, the scantily clad "Elaine." [18]

Yet humorous rituals could not mask the anxiety of growing up in the atomic age. Even optimism about Dwight Eisenhower's visionary 1953 "Atoms for Peace" program was accompanied by expressions of fear and hedged with a sense of the disappointing past. Lafayette's poet laureate, for example, yearned for a "better era," in which "the dread atom bomb / Shall give to industry its helpful service in a world of calm." Faced with a future that was neither knowable nor secure, the author of the dedication of the 1955 Burgard *Craftsman* found sustenance in religion, offering a prayer "that the destructive forces of the atomic weapons will be converted to peace and benevolence and that the ever present hand of God will guide and protect us in this menacing age." [19]

Despite these anxieties, postwar middle-class youth appeared remarkably and intensely optimistic, convinced (or at least willing to write in the yearbooks as if they were) that every problem had its solution and that progress—political, social, and personal—depended on what they thought and did. As bleak as the world seemed, yearbook illustrators sketched cities of the future, reminiscent of the 1939 World's Fair; a harmonious urban tomorrow, under the new sun of

atomic power; rockets that launched graduates into the twenty-first century; and schools that stood for, and dispensed, skill, power, and knowledge.[20]

Buffalo's idealistic students remained confident that a solution had been found for the conflicts of religion, race, and nationalism that they supposed lay at the heart of World War II and the Cold War. Just as an earlier generation had vested its dream of ending war in a piece of paper called the Kellogg-Briand Pact (1928), Cold War youth took refuge in a secular religion called the United Nations. Throughout the late 1940s and 1950s, the United Nations was the subject of assembly programs and yearbook dedications, and each year dozens of the city's students took part in a Model General Assembly. Photographs of the UN's international-style New York headquarters were thought sufficiently inspiring for yearbook reproduction. Riverside yearbook editors warned that survival itself was at stake. "If it fails," they wrote, "our civilization must crumble."[21]

The Politics of Hair. A talented cartoonist for the Lafayette *Oracle* understood that the brush cut was part of the structure of authority as well as a simple hairstyle. *Oracle, 1948.*

Seneca Vocational,
Chieftain, 1952.

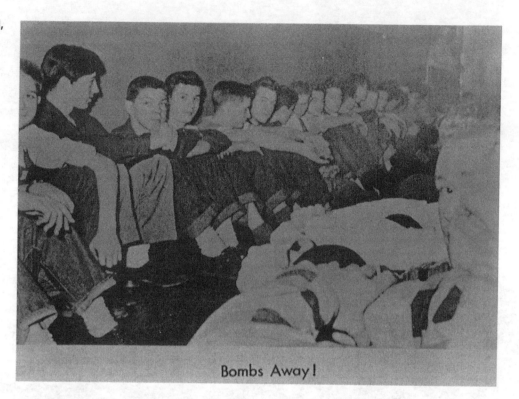

Bombs Away!

Elaine—Our Answer
to Sputnik (Riverside
Skipper, 1958).

Students may have
sensed that in an
atomic age, Elaine
was as likely to con-
tribute to survival as
a civil defense drill.

After five years of world war and the use of the first atomic weapons, students remained optimistic about the future and convinced, as this artist must have been, that even the vocational schools would foster abundant opportunity. Buffalo Technical, *Techtonian*, 1946.

MUSIC

In describing the culture of their youth, those who were teenagers in Buffalo in the 1940s and 1950s stress the importance of music, style, dress, and the organizations to which they belonged. Because these categories stretch across class, ethnicity, and race, one can argue for the existence of a youth culture linked by certain basic commonalities. Indeed, some of the most important experiences of postwar youth, such as the "Hi-Teen" program discussed below, tend to be remembered as synonymous with coming of age in Buffalo, as if they touched and affected all youth, equally. What is less easily recognized and understood, and what therefore requires historical understanding, is that even the most popular manifestations of youth culture were also, and perhaps essentially, biased by class, race, gender, and other categories that could not be compromised. The problem can be put another way. If middle-class white youth were dancing to Bill Haley's version of "Shake, Rattle and Roll" in one section of the city, and working-class black youth to Joe Turner's version in another, is it reasonable or sufficient to argue the existence of a single, unified "youth culture"?

A second issue concerns the extent to which youth were responsible for the creation of the culture they remember as their own. The oral histories present youth as subjects—going, joining, dancing, listening, doing. Although this collective memory may accurately describe the formation of a fraternity or sorority, it does not fully explain "Hi-Teen," a social-engineering venture from the beginning. To a considerable degree, youths were the objects of middle-class, adult efforts to shape and contain youth culture and subcultures.

The musical culture of postwar youth was extraordinarily diverse. Its major components included the disc jockey, dancing, records, live performances, and intense consumer and fan loyalties. Several major changes occurred in this musical culture in the fifteen years after 1945, including the rise of rock 'n' roll; the emergence of the 45 rpm record as the industry's standard; and the gradual development of the recorded, rather than the live, performance as the quintessential musical experience.

The 45 rpm record was both a representation of the desire of capitalists to penetrate and profit from the youth market and an artifact of the new youth culture. In 1945, recorded music was available only in the large and brittle 78 rpm format. The 45 rpm record was introduced in 1949 and became the industry stan-

Machines like this one, designed to play only 45 rpm records, testified to youth's attraction to the new, unbreakable, and easily portable 45s. Courtesy of the Buffalo and Erie County Historical Society, copyright 1986.

dard in the mid-1950s, so that it was soon possible to purchase a record player that would play *only* at the 45 rpm speed. Four-speed machines belonged to an earlier shaking-out period, before the industry settled on 45 and 33⅓ as its two basic recording speeds. Unlike the 78s, the new 45s were strong, portable (especially in the cases designed just for them), and ideally suited to mobile youth. The machines, too, quickly became portable, and teenagers enjoyed putting the machine, and playing the records, where they wanted to.[22]

The best evidence for the existence of a youth culture is the amount of media energy devoted to it. The war had been over only a year when WEBR, a middle-of-the-road station owned by the *Buffalo Courier-Express*, went on the air with a program called "Hi-Teen." For fifteen years—until 1961, when the program went off the air—its emcee and guiding spirit was Bob Wells. Like many of those who programmed popular music for youth in the 1940s and 1950s, Wells had adult musical preferences; in fact, his own musical training was in classical flute. But Wells "could sell anything," as his assistant recalled, and Hi-Teen enjoyed a large and appreciative audience. Hi-Teen dances, broadcast live on Saturday afternoons from the Delwood Ballroom on Main Street at Utica, drew crowds of three hundred to two thousand youths, all card-carrying members of the Hi-Teen Club, an organization created by the station to promote the program and to manage the teenagers. Membership in the club reached 22,000 by 1954. In 1949, *Billboard Magazine* rated "Hi-Teen" the third most popular record show in the United States.

In January 1949, hundreds of Hi-Teen Club members paid a special admission charge to attend a "March of Dime-ers" dance. Such events were designed to encourage social responsibility among teenagers, to counter juvenile delinquency, and, as this photograph reveals, to encourage young people to want an automobile. Courtesy, Bob Wells.

Hi-Teen producers tried to steer teenagers away from bebop, rhythm and blues, and rock 'n' roll and toward traditional crooners such as Perry Como, shown here signing autographs. Bob Wells, Hi-Teen's emcee, is in the background. C. 1949. Courtesy, Bob Wells.

Many area youths look back fondly on those Saturday afternoons at the Delwood. But it is well to remember that "Hi-Teen" was a show with a social purpose. It was designed by adults to "contain" juvenile delinquency. To accomplish this, the show directed much of its attention to defining and promoting appropriate teenage behavior. Thus Hi-Teen Club members found themselves enlisted in the March of Dimes or collecting food for Europe's hungry masses.[23] Through a regular series of Teen-of-the-Month contests, Hi-Teen Club members were rewarded for having "perfect feet" or well-cared-for teeth.

"Hi-Teen" producers were especially conscious of shaping teenage taste in music. Although the program's ratings made possible a star-studded guest list, those who performed on the "Hi-Teen" bandstand were often artists booked into Buffalo's Town Casino, a popular Main Street nightclub with a predominately adult clientele. As a result, the typical celebrity at Hi-Teen was from the mainstream of American popular music, and many, including Tony Martin, Vic Damone, Benny Goodman, and Lionel Hampton, made their strongest appeal to an audience that was white, middle class, and adult. Rhythm and blues and, after 1954, rock 'n' roll, were seldom heard on the "Hi-Teen" stage. In consequence, Hi-Teen's audience was surely no cross section of Buffalo. The city's private-school elite did not attend, nor did most blacks, nor the tougher elements of the working class. A working-class girl, whose friends wore sequined Elvis Presley jackets and preferred Chuck Berry to Pat Boone, had this response to Hi-Teen: "we didn't bother with anyone who went up to the Delwood."

And what did all this have to do with the containment of juvenile delinquency? Just this: Hi-Teen could not eradicate delinquency; it could not prevent vandalism, car theft, or gang fights. What it could do was to teach its core audience of middle-class white youth what "good" popular music was and wasn't and, at the same time, keep the delinquent elements out of the "ballroom." Such policies would not eliminate delinquency at its source, but they could contain it—that is, keep it from spreading to the middle class.

Those who were turned away at the Delwood or who yearned for a more visceral and exciting music than that presented to Hi-Teen audiences would find a hero of their own in George "Hound Dog" Lorenz. In a few short years in the mid-1950s, Lorenz went from obscurity to fame as one of the nation's premier rhythm and blues and rock 'n' roll disc jockeys.

In 1951, "Ol' Man Lorenz," as he was then known, was programming rhythm and blues over WJJL in Niagara Falls, New York, while promoting country and western shows in the Tonawandas. "Hound Dog" (the name is derived from the 1940s expression "doggin' around") would build a brief contact with an unknown Elvis Presley into a minor but significant career relationship, "breaking out" Presley's 1954 recording of "Mystery Train" and bringing the singer to Buffalo for an auditorium concert in 1957. The qualities that Lorenz must have seen in young Presley—energy, bravado, a certain easy familiarity with black culture—were precisely the ones that the Hound would parlay into one of the most successful radio shows in the Northeast.

When Lorenz arrived in Buffalo, WGR had been experimenting with programming black music. "Record Barbecue," a mixture of progressive jazz and "spiritualistic" blues emceed by Buffalo's first "Negro" disc jockey, James A. "Ducky" Rice, went on the air in the spring of 1953. But Rice's audience was no doubt avant-garde, while Lorenz would attempt to merge significant portions of white and black cultures. He got the chance in 1955, when Burt and Ralph Glaser bought the Zanzibar Lounge at William and Monroe Streets, a Harlemlike neighborhood, and converted it into an interracial club (audiences were roughly 20 percent black) featuring Fats Domino, Bill Haley, Little Richard, Lloyd Price, LaVerne Baker, and other big-name R&B and rock 'n' roll artists. Lorenz was brought in to broadcast live, at first from the Zanzibar stage, later from a "Doghouse" booth built specially for him. By mid-1956, the Hound was broadcasting six nights a week over WKBW and promoting stage-show extravaganzas at the auditorium, while the Hound Dog Fan Club had more than five hundred chapters along the East Coast and a newsletter, "The Hound-Dog's Howl." So successful was Lorenz—and so confident of his place in popular music—that he attempted

The typical Hi-Teener was white and middle class. Perhaps they were the only ones who would tolerate the Bunny Hop. 1952. Courtesy, Bob Wells. *(opposite page)*

A Saturday afternoon at the Delwood Ballroom, early 1950s. Courtesy, Bob Wells.

The Sub-Deb club modeling at Hi-Teen. Courtesy, Bob Wells. "The fashion show," writes a woman who was among the models that day, "was an exception to the usual avoidance that 'our crowd' from [the suburb of] Williamsville exercised toward Hi-Teen; mostly because our parents confused it with the evangelical 'Youth for Christ' organization, which was antithetical to the staid religious practices of people in Williamsville, and because they were also concerned that we would pick up radical ideas from these kids whose parents they didn't know. . . . Fact is, we in Williamsville didn't need organized efforts like Hi-Teen and the dress code; everyone in the village *knew* how to behave."

Hi-Teen was formally organized as a "club." The programs were called "meetings," and the meetings were routinely opened with group singing of the club theme song. Wallet-size cards like this one, complete with rules on the back, were first issued in 1947 when the program moved to the Elks Club. One rule limited membership to youths under sixteen; another prohibited entering any part of the Elks building except the ballroom and the attached restrooms. Courtesy, Bob Wells.

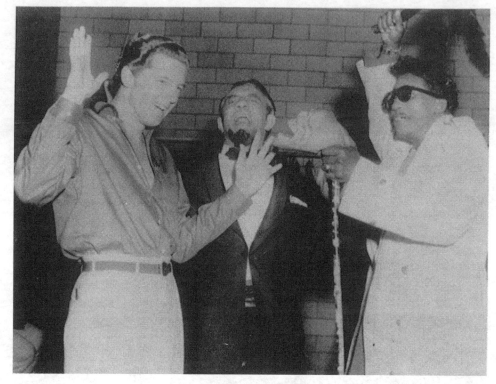

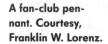

A fan-club pennant. Courtesy, Franklin W. Lorenz.

The Hound joins Jerry Lee Lewis and Screamin' Jay Hawkins. Hawkins' stage persona had been identified with the iconography of death since the day in 1956 when he emerged from a coffin to open a performance at New York's Paramount Theater. C. 1957. Courtesy, Franklin W. Lorenz.

to mark off a big-beat, tuneful, lyrically "clean" music and to distinguish it from rock 'n' roll with his own term, "movin' and groovin.'"[24]

It is difficult to imagine the intensity with which Buffalo youths responded to Lorenz in the mid-1950s. One mailed in a self-portrait of a young boy, ear pressed to the radio, linked to the Hound by an airwave. But what was the source of this devotion? Besides talent—and Lorenz certainly had that—the Hound touched Buffalo teens in two important ways. First, he was an iconoclast in an age of conformity, an inspiration for those youths, mostly working class, who felt trapped by an unyielding dominant culture. One of the Hound's biggest fans recalls an evening when the disc jockey came into the Deco restaurant at Fillmore and Box Streets, wearing the purple "drapes" (trousers) that instantly marked one as a social rebel. "When we saw him, we put Elvis's 'Hound Dog' on the jukebox. There was this square sitting at the counter, and, looking at the Hound's clothes, he says 'What's this, a centennial or something?' The Hound says, 'He just doesn't understand, does he?'"[25]

The second reason for the Hound's enthusiastic following has to do with race. Lorenz was at the center of a complex set of relationships between white and

This photograph was taken at the Shrine Teen Canteen, which opened at the Hadji Temple at 118 East Utica Street in February 1955. The canteen was explicitly interracial, and those attending were required to pledge their intent to behave "in an orderly manner and to be a good neighbor." As the photograph indicates, the function drew more blacks than whites. Courtesy, Franklin W. Lorenz.

black cultures. Though white, Lorenz was responsible for transmitting the energy and sexuality of black culture to white teenagers. Besides programming black music, he regularly referred to himself as "the big round brown Hound," used a "jive hip talk" adapted from black language patterns, and, according to one source, lived in the black community. His Zanzibar broadcasts attracted inter-racial audiences—a Burgard Vocational student recalls going to the club with a group of white and black friends—and his auditorium promotions were usually interracial events, attended by blacks and whites who sat side by side to watch a racially mixed card.[26] Although there was racial conflict between white and black teenagers throughout the 1950s, Hound Dog represented the possibility of an interracial community based on a shared black youth subculture.

"You can rock it you can roll it / you can bop it you can stroll it." In the fall of 1957, following the release of Danny and the Juniors' number-one hit "At the Hop," almost every American adolescent knew where all this activity took place, and the "hop" soon came to symbolize the swirling frenzy of dancing teenage America.

In Buffalo, the "record hop"—by definition, an event at which dancing takes place to recorded music—probably dates to the first "Hi-Teen" program in 1946. But as a phenomenon of historical importance, it belongs to the late-1950s period of conservatism and retrenchment in popular music. In Buffalo, the retreat from rock 'n' roll was well under way by 1957, when WGR radio declared itself "out of the rock 'n' roll field" and announced its intention to follow a "sweet music formula" with records by Pat Boone, Bing Crosby, and Perry Como. At WKBW, only the Hound held out against the official trend toward "playing down the 'big beat.'" That April, *Courier-Express* reporter Margaret Wynn described Elvis Presley, performing on the stage of Memorial Auditorium, as resembling "a young man with a troubled digestive system. . . . strutting on the stage like the gawky teen-agers he entrances." "It is purely personal prejudice," added the editorial staff at the *News*, "that causes us to flee the premises when Mr. Elvis Presley's tones are emitted by juke box or phonograph." Buffalo teenagers were just a step behind the media, voting Presley male vocalist of the year in 1957 but selecting Como the following year.[27]

Record hops were for middle-class, mostly white teenagers—a substantial majority of them young girls—who were not attuned to hard-core rock 'n' roll or rhythm and blues. One version of the genre was WBEN's "Statler Hop," hosted

In the mid-1950s, disc jockeys had much the same celebrity status as recording artists. Lorenz had devoted followers all along the East Coast. Here, a fan displays his collection. Courtesy, Franklin W. Lorenz.

COMING! COMING!

Another Great Entertainment Event

HOUND DOG and SUPER Attractions present

Sun., OCT. 28-8.30 pm MEMORIAL AUDITORIUM Main and Terrace, Buffalo, N. Y.
ALL SEATS RESERVED $1.50, $2.00, $2.50, $3.00, $3.50 Including Tax

MAIL ORDERS ACCEPTED—Send Remittance—Make Payable to BIGGEST SHOW CO. and Mail to TICKET OFFICE Denton, Cottier
& Daniels, 32 Court Street, Buffalo 2, N. Y. TICKETS ON SALE STARTING MONDAY OCTOBER 15
At Denton, Cottier & Daniels, and all Cavages Record Stores.

This same great show will also appear at AUDITORIUM THEATRE, ROCHESTER, N. Y.
FRIDAY, OCTOBER 26—2 BIG SHOWS—7 P.M. AND 10 P.M.

Keller Bros. Miller Printers, 401 Franklin St., Buffalo, N. Y.

Before the Canadiana riot of 1956 changed Buffalo race relations, white and black youths often attended the same clubs, films, and performances.

The Hound's auditorium promotions drew blacks and whites. C. 1957. Courtesy, Franklin W. Lorenz.

Buffalo's black middle class at the Town Casino, 1952. Courtesy, Mary Carter.

Lorenz was a promoter as well as a disc jockey. This card describes an October 28, 1956, show in Memorial Auditorium. Courtesy, Franklin W. Lorenz.

Bennett High
School's Commu-
nity Association, a
parent organization,
sponsored the Hal-
loween Hop, and
the yearbook editors
experimented with
irony, 1959. *Bea-
con*, commencement
issue.

Fun at the Hop

by Van Miller and first aired in September 1957 from the elegant Rendezvous
Room at the Statler Hotel. Miller recalls that the audience, made up each week
of selected students from one area high school, was well behaved ("the rowdies
probably did not show up"), well dressed, and so homogeneous that it was a
problem finding interesting things to talk about. The music played on "Statler
Hop" was that of Bobby Rydell, Connie Francis, Bobby Vinton, and other "teen
idols" who were on the popular fringe of rock 'n' roll and whose music suggested
romance rather than sex. "It was," the music librarian for the show erroneously
yet significantly remembers, "a little early for rock 'n' roll."[28]

The most significant series of Buffalo record hops was that broadcast by WEBR
and hosted by disc jockeys Ed Little, Bernie Sandler, and, especially, Danny
McBride, Jr. Raised in a working-class neighborhood of South Buffalo, McBride
cut his broadcasting teeth at the Babcock Boys Club, where, in the early 1950s,
he and Danny Neaverth wired the club for closed-circuit coverage of sport-
ing events and did their own versions of national shows such as Don McNeil's
"Breakfast Club."

In the late-1950s heyday of the record hop, McBride was host for thousands of hops, broadcast live every weekday evening from places like the Big Tree Fire Hall on South Park Avenue, St. Peter and Paul's Church Hall in Hamburg, St. Lucy's Auditorium on Swan Street, the Lackawanna Recreation Hall, and McKinley High School. Because the hops were for the station a way of promoting its disc jockeys, WEBR did not charge admission for the events, which included hot dogs for three hundred and soft drinks, courtesy of Pepsi-Cola.[29]

Hot dogs and Pepsi, McBride and his crewcut, sponsors that included Our Mother of Good Council branch of the Catholic Youth Council, neighborhood locations, and the tepid popular music of the late 1950s, selected by the media —in most respects, the record hop was a conservative, community-sanctioned institution. McBride was applauded by the YMCA for providing the kind of "wholesome recreation" for teenagers that would keep them "out of trouble." Although black teens now and then attended some of the WEBR record hops, generally the event held little appeal for Buffalo's blacks. As McBride recalls, "We never had requests to go into an all-black neighborhood."[30]

This is not to say that the hop was entirely a product of the social-engineering desires of the dominant capitalist culture. The institution had intrinsic appeal for those teenagers—generally young, middle class, and female—who desired some distance or protection from the physical culture of the street, the musical culture of rock 'n' roll, or the aggressive sexuality of boys. The hop was also in some sense a concession to youth culture, a compromise formation that existed only because youth had in no uncertain terms announced its rejection of the popular musical tradition of Tin Pan Alley. Nonetheless, the record hop was an exceedingly limited institution. While claiming to represent all teenagers, the hop was actually designed to set a certain group apart from the most threatening aspects (male, working class, black) of the new youth culture.

Even when sponsored by the schools, record hops at least offered a segment of youths a taste of something resembling their own musical culture. In contrast, high school music programs restricted student access to varieties of music that were strongly identified with youth. Record and "disc" clubs, many of them formed in the decade after 1945, were a concession to student interest in music. But they were invariably structured less to allow an outlet for the folk culture of youth than to stimulate an appreciation of the big band, the Hollywood musical, and the classical genres deemed safe and socially responsible by adults. At recently integrated East High School, few blacks belonged to a disc club where

"popular" music meant songs from *Oklahoma!*, *South Pacific*, and other stage and film productions. At working-class Burgard Vocational High School, where rhythm and blues and rock 'n' roll had a strong following among students, the administration ignored this new music in its obsession to demonstrate "that a vocational school can and will support the highest forms of culture." East High principal William H. Davenport explained the role of music in the postwar high school while commenting on the selection of "music" as the theme of the 1958 yearbook. "Good music," wrote Davenport, "should appeal to the noble emotions; it should aid us in the quest for the good, the true and the beautiful." Insisting that parents and teachers did not "condemn all modern music," Davenport labeled some modern compositions "excellent," others representative of the time and "enjoyable," and a few "combinations of rhythmic noise and ghoulish howls. Do not be prejudiced against any particular type of music," he concluded. "Listen with an open mind and receptive heart. Accept what appeals to your sense of the good, the beautiful and the true."[31]

Hi-Teen, the Hound, the hop, the school disc club—each was in some measure an attempt to come to terms with dramatic changes in the musical preferences of teenagers and with the implications of those changes for the dominant culture. That they did so in such different ways—Davenport railing against the very forms that Lorenz so much admired—suggests differences and divisions within the ranks of the dominant culture over the nature of the challenge as well as over possible responses to it. At one end of the spectrum, Hi Teen and the hop advocated some version of cultural segregation, hoping to isolate middle-class youth from outside influences; at the other end, the Hound called for integration, setting his sights on a culture invigorated by the infusion of subcultural forms.[32]

One could argue, then, that for as long as the Hound stuck to his guns (and it was not long before even he rejected the term "rock 'n' roll" for one of his own invention, "movin' 'n' groovin'"), the dominant culture itself had room for the more confrontational subcultural music. One could also argue, however, that the number, variety, and swiftness of responses to rock 'n' roll and rhythm and blues are evidence of the extraordinary energy given over to containing and incorporating the new meanings and values being created by an incipient counterculture. "Indeed it is significant in our own period," writes Raymond Williams, "how very early this attempt is, how alert the dominant culture now is to anything that can be seen as emergent. . . . In capitalist practice, if the thing is not making a profit,

970 ★ WEBR ★ 970

RECORD HOP

BIG TREE FIRE HALL
SOUTH PARK AVENUE

August 11, 1958

8:00 to 11:00 p.m.
ADMISSION 90c

☆ GUEST STARS ☆

Come Kids ☆ Refreshments *It's Going*
☆ Door Prizes *to be Great*
☆ Loads of Fun

Sponsored by
OUR MOTHER OF GOOD COUNCIL C.Y.C.

Churches and church organizations were regular sponsors of record hops, an adult-sanctioned aspect of youth culture. Courtesy, Danny McBride, Jr.

Danny McBride, Jr., the king of Buffalo record-hop disc jockeys, joins teens in a hot dog and Pepsi-Cola, c. 1958. The position of the soft drink and McBride's prominence illustrate commercial and media penetration of youth culture. Courtesy, Danny McBride, Jr.

A cartoonist's view of the conflict over music. The band director has chosen "Sleigh Ride"; the zoot-suited rebel at left, complete with Mexican hat and keychain, prefers the rhythm and blues number "Night Train." Buffalo Technical, *Techtonian*, 1956.

She did, and she didn't. Burgard *Craftsman*, 1958.

or if it is not being widely circulated, then it can for some time be overlooked, at least while it remains alternative."[33] The new music was making a profit; it was being widely circulated; and it was not being overlooked.

STYLE

The critical place of clothing and style in postwar youth culture was assured in the zoot suit riots of June 1943, when sailors invaded the Mexican section of Los Angeles in search of "zooters" (the costume included flared trousers, a broad felt hat, and a keychain with a pocket knife). Those who were caught had their pants removed and their "Argentine ducktail" haircuts trimmed. Throughout the postwar period, fashions and style expressed a variety of youth "folk" subcultures, and sometimes challenged the hegemony of the dominant culture.[34]

The zoot suit's influence on Buffalo's youth culture can be seen in the "pegged pants" or "drapes" (the terms refer roughly to the same garment) that were popular largely among working-class youth into the mid-1950s. The basic style was not in itself countercultural. Some "squares" wore drapes, as did white "hipsters" out to flaunt an unaccepted style. One could tell the square from the hipster by fabric, color, and cut. Hipsters had their drapes cut in sharkskin or mohair, and often in pink, chartreuse, rust, or powder blue, and the taper of the trouser was notably extreme—from a twenty-four-inch knee down to a fourteen-inch cuff. (Some blacks wore even more sharply tapered drapes.) Belt loops were "dropped" two and sometimes three inches from the waist. One could apparently purchase drapes off the rack at downtown department stores, but the more extreme hipster look could be achieved only by having the pants made by hand at Ray Spasiano's on Ferry Street or at Sam "the wailin' tailor" (as the Hound referred to him) on South Park Avenue. Having their clothes tailored to personal specifications suggests the degree to which some youths desired, and were able, to remain independent of fashion industry efforts to commodify and co-opt subcultural styles. Similar motives led other youths to customize automobiles.[35]

Other clothing customs were noticeable among postwar Buffalo teenagers. Among middle-class white youths (pejoratively, "squares" or "squeaks"), chinos or khakis (a word with a military connotation) were the norm for boys, as were vertically striped sport shirts (standing for "dependability and rectitude"), V-neck

Relatively few youths had automobiles in the 1950s. Those who did often customized their vehicles, in the process investing the product of capitalism with elements of the folk culture of youth. Bo Kreiger applied a zebra interior to his 1946 Mercury. C. 1953. Courtesy, Jerry Szefel.

The lowered belt loops, billowy knees, and sharp below-the-knee taper were characteristics of the "drapes" worn by Ronny Scinta (*right*) and thousands of other Buffalo youth in the late 1940s and early 1950s. C. 1950. Courtesy, Gail Whitman.

Something of the stylish defiance of the Los Angeles zoot-suiters was captured in this photograph of Jim Boettcher in a Sun-day suit, taken in the Fillmore/East Utica area of the city's East Side. C. 1958. Courtesy, Jerry Szefel.

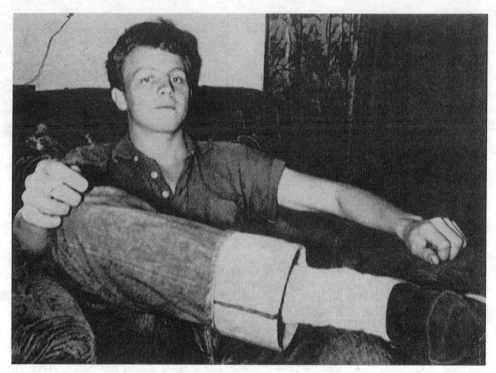

You could do anything except step on his blue suede shoes. C. 1953. Courtesy, Gail Whitman.

sweaters, and dress shirts with button-down collars.[36] Working-class boys were fond of checked flannel shirts (appropriate to farming, hunting, logging, and camping), sweatshirts, and—especially after James Dean's 1955 performance in *Rebel Without a Cause*—levis.

Culture and politics, fashion and one's attitude toward authority were often inseparable. At Seneca Vocational, for example, a 1956 graduate best noted for wearing "white bucks" also had a crewcut, was a member of the Civil Defense Committee, had been on the honor roll eighteen times, and had achieved a perfect attendance record as a sophomore and junior. The combination of extreme drapes, a shirt with a "Mr. B." (Billy Eckstine) collar, black or blue suede shoes (tied with pink or chartreuse shoelaces) was sufficient to irritate police, school administrators, Hi-Teen Club supervisors, juvenile court judges, or parents, and to qualify one as a social rebel. Parents and public officials were offended in part because certain modes of dress were clearly devised as a form of opposition to constituted authority, and in part because certain aspects of the style described above were adapted from, or modeled after, black culture.[37] The wearing

The American Tough, 1953. Although *Life* had described jeans in 1949 as a "national teenage uniform," many youths refused to wear them. According to one recollection, "levis were for farmers." For Mike Sendlbeck (foreground), posing on Fillmore Avenue, it was "Wranglers, not Levis. You had to have Wranglers with the cuffs rolled up." Courtesy, Mike Sendlbeck.

Typical late 1940s neckties. By 1960, ties would be narrower, less colorful, and less creative in design. Courtesy of the Buffalo and Erie County Historical Society, copyright 1986.

of large, brightly colored, and elaborately designed ties was, on the other hand, an adult-sanctioned youth custom of the late 1940s and early 1950s.

Girls expressed bonds of friendship and fraternity by sharing items of clothing or wearing identical outfits. "All of us girls used to switch," a woman recalls. "You had to wear it first yourself, of course." A standard outfit for girls at Buffalo Seminary, Bennett High School, and other institutions for the elite or upwardly mobile middle class consisted of a plaid skirt, a plain blouse or sweater, white socks, and dirty saddle shoes. Because the poodle signified the elite world, there was some hostility among working-class girls toward the poodle skirt. "We didn't all wear poodle skirts, I'll tell you that," recalled one woman. "We all had *felt* skirts, is what we had."[38]

Chronological and social patterns in youth jackets can shed light on certain aspects of youth culture. Throughout the period, most jackets were manufactured in corduroy. In the mid-1950s, however, in response to Marlon Brando's performance as the leader of a motorcycle club, the leather jacket took a significant share of the market, reflecting a new, more confrontational youth culture and the growing interest of middle-class youth in working-class style. Colors and fabrics also changed. In the mid-1940s Broadway Knitting Mills, the largest Buffalo manufacturer of youth jackets, introduced its famous zebra- and leopard-trimmed corduroy jacket, and began to trim other jackets in chartreuse, shrimp, and powder blue. Though the early 1950s brought the introduction of the pink and black jacket, the decade would be decidedly less colorful than its predecessor. Changes also took place in how the jackets were labeled, changes that in turn suggest changing patterns of membership and loyalty. In the 1940s and 1950s, Broadway Knitting Mills did a significant business in jackets for high school fraternities and sororities and neighborhood gangs and clubs, including the Cobraettes, the Da Boys, the Rollin' Injuns (a roller skating group), the Crazy Sounds, and the Savants. After 1960, as the more local, spontaneous, and self-created loyalties that had spawned these organizations were replaced or overshadowed by loyalty to the high school, the jackets changed too, until most were decorated only with an institutional affiliation.[39]

The checked flannel shirts worn by these Buffalo Technical students were especially favored by working-class youth. *Techtonian*, 1954.

Margaret Barwell and Dorothy Zuercher, photographed in Williamsville at one stop of their frequent bicycle excursions out of the city. C. 1950. Girls expressed bonds of friendship by sharing items of clothing or wearing identical outfits. Courtesy, Dorothy Gallagher.

White girls pose at Girls Vocational High School, 1953. Boyish nicknames —Butch, Willie, Donnie, Buster, Wally—were common at vocational schools for girls. Courtesy, Dorothy Gallagher.

Senior-class officers at Buffalo Seminary display their saddle shoes. *Seminaria*, 1952. A certain calculated sloppiness (here, within a context of order) was, and remains, a characteristic of elite subculture. For a further understanding of social class, compare the precise presentation in this photograph with the more organic style in the photograph opposite below.

ORGANIZATIONS

The dominance of the high school in the lives of young people, a dominance marked by the Beach Boys' 1963 single, "Be True to Your School," was much more pronounced by the mid-1960s than it had been two decades earlier. Yet Buffalo's youth culture as an organizational phenomenon remained heavily influenced by ethnicity, neighborhood, religion, race, and class. Although many Buffalo teenagers participated in the CYO (Catholic Youth Organization), Hi-Y (the youth arm of the YMCA and YWCA), Boys Clubs, and other organizations created by adults and often lodged in the schools, others remained in control of their culture by creating and perpetuating their own organizations. Two kinds of youth-generated organizations—gangs and clubs, and fraternities and sororities—deserve special attention.

To Buffalo's police and press, every bunch of kids was a "gang," and therefore threatening. The word "gang" was applied indiscriminately to street-corner loungers, vandals, neighborhood clubs, groups of roving teenagers, groups with and without names or jackets, and—most legitimately—to groups of youths organized for, or prone to, violence, conflict, and crime.

Even by this definition, postwar Buffalo had numerous gangs. On the city's West Side, gangs called the Rebels and the Yankees, and wearing gray and blue caps, fought each other in the Grant Street area. By the early 1960s, the Warlords were operating in the Fruit Belt region and the Willert Projects had produced the Projecteers. Both were black. The Aces, an early-1950s gang made up of thirteen- to fourteen-year-old boys in the vicinity of Fillmore and Main, apparently made its reputation by stealing cars and joyriding. The Broadway-Fillmore area had the Bebops and the Dudes, allegedly involved in a series of home burglaries. Genesee and Montana was the scene of a 1954 "pitched battle over girls" between two unnamed gangs of fifteen-year-olds, one representing the east side of Bailey Avenue, the other the west side. Even the staid, close-in suburb of Kenmore had gangs, specialists, it would seem, in stripping cars in the parking lot of the Colvin Theater. Girl gangs—of which little is known—included the Embraceables, the El Dorados, the Queens, and the Conservative Lovers. Some gangs carried weapons, more commonly at the end of the period than the beginning. In 1960, for example, police who headed off a clash between youths near Abbott Road and Meriden Street in South Buffalo confiscated nineteen weapons, including seven baseball bats (two sawed off), two lug wrenches, a pitchfork, a

From "Down on the Levee," a Catholic Youth Council production staged in 1947 by high school youth at St. Margaret's, a North Buffalo grammar school. Despite such efforts to maintain control of youth culture, many teenagers belonged to organizations that were largely independent of adult authority. Courtesy, Thomas Owen.

pickaxe, and a car transmission spline, described by a police captain as "the worst such weapon I've ever seen."[40]

By far the most famous confrontation in Buffalo's postwar gang history involved two white gangs, the Gunners and the Park Gang (also known as the North Fillmore Gang). The Park Gang was made up of Polish teenagers from the Humboldt Park area. The Gunners—Irish, Hungarian, and German—hailed from the vicinity of Masten and Dodge Streets, just north of what was then Fosdick-Masten Park High School. The Gunners' jackets—chartreuse corduroy trimmed in black, embossed with 45-caliber pistols—reflected the gang's reputation for style, loyalty, and violence. Other gangs, one woman recalls, "mingled with other kids . . . the Gunners were Gunners first." Another woman remembers the Gunners as "really nice guys. My mother and father would sit on the porch in front of our house and the Gunners would walk down the street with a lead pipe on the way to a 'rumble,' and they'd always stop and say hello to my mother and father."[41]

On an early September day in 1953, the Gunners greeted their neighbors and headed north and east toward their rumble with the Park Gang, hoping to avenge

Spain's 1972 rendering of the legendary battle between the Gunners and the Park Gang captures the event as an exceedingly violent and yet downright enjoyable moment in history. The Sedita poster displayed on the wall (center) probably refers to Judge Frank A. Sedita, in whose courtroom eight participants were found guilty. Although blacks were present, the confrontation was by no means a racial one. The actual event took place in September 1953. Used with the permission of the artist. The copyright remains in the ownership of Manuel (Spain) Rodriguez.

an injury to a Gunner suffered in a confrontation with the same gang earlier in the week. The Park Gang had beefed up its forces with recruits from the Apaches, a black gang. The confrontation, recreated in a 1972 sketch by Buffalo artist Spain, took place on Fillmore between Box and North Parade. "We all went," recalls one woman. "I remember Teddy leaning against that lamp post. We told him he better run because the cops were coming. Then we realized he was hand-cuffed to the lamp post." Two youths were injured, neither seriously, and sixteen were booked on charges of disorderly conduct. Eight youths, all of whom pleaded innocent, were found guilty by city judge Frank A. Sedita, well known for his "firm" stand on matters related to youth conduct. Although the fight is remembered by participants as extraordinarily violent—the quintessential rumble—the recollection of a neighborhood girl may be more accurate. "We all went over to watch," she recalls. "I don't think anyone was hurt."[42]

Less threatening to the social order were Buffalo's numerous neighborhood clubs. One example is the Lucky Bucs, a "good gang" created in 1953 in the Cold Spring territory of the Gunners. The Lucky Bucs wore green jackets bearing a deer with dice between its antlers. They played cards and other games and, though regularly driven from the street corners by the police, left shoplifting and similar acts of delinquency to others. Equally pacific were the Peruvians, whose name was derived from the street (near Bailey and Dingens) on which many of its members lived. Because the Polish and German neighborhood of some thirty homes was physically isolated, conflicts with other gangs or clubs never materialized, and the club turned inward, developing an unusual intimacy. As a former Peruvian recalls, "There was a lot of communication."[43]

Girls also formed clubs. Fan clubs, formed in devotion to a movie star or singer, offered girls a relatively passive experience, romantic rather than sexual and distanced from the more aggressive and street-based male subcultures. A group of girls in the vicinity of Michigan Avenue and Offerman Stadium wore hip-length black jackets with zebra-striped sleeves and a sequined "Elvis Presley" and the name of a favorite Presley song on the back. The group remained nameless because "we didn't want anybody to call us a gang. We all had trouble with our parents. . . . They didn't like us hanging around." On the East Side, black girls established the Jackie Wilson Fan Club in 1952. The Saints, centered at Skateland in the Main-Utica area, was composed of roller-skating enthusiasts from several sections of the city; some considered the club an appendage of the

Gunners. (According to Erik Erikson, the name "Saints," like other historical references, demonstrates a group's deluded claim to have its own traditions and ethics.)[44]

The city's largest gang or club was the Black Ts, whose members wore black T-shirts on the streets and to school. The club was created in 1954 or 1955 at the Regal Restaurant, at Playter and Broadway. Robert Depczynski, the gang's leader throughout its three-year history, had purchased several black T-shirts because "they looked good on us." At its peak, the two major branches of the Black Ts, one to the west of Fillmore, the other to the east, could muster anywhere from a hundred to a thousand members (estimates vary), each screened by Depczynski and tested in a wrestling match with the leader. Although the great majority of the members were Polish, "there was one black," recalls Depczynski; "we called him Spook." Girls from the neighborhood, for whom the wrestling requirement was presumably waived, had their own branch of the Black Ts. The

The Dukes AC, a West Side social club, managed this photograph with Marilyn Monroe during the filming of *Niagara* in 1952. Created by high school students, the Dukes remained active until its members moved to the suburbs. Courtesy, Frank A. Palombaro, Sr.

The Jackie Wilson Fan Club, in pink and black, 1953. The club was organized in the Jefferson/William area. Courtesy, Johnnie M. Mayo.

Members of the Saints, a small girls' club founded at Skateland on Main Street in about 1950. Courtesy, Gail Whitman.

Black Ts held street dances and picnics, frequented the Sweet Spot, a soda shop on Broadway near Sweet Avenue, hung around street corners, did some drinking, and gathered on weekends in larger numbers at the Central Terminal or at Dold's Playground at Fillmore and William. On Sunday mornings, Depcynzski and his friends drove through the city listening to polkas. Though the Ts "never had any fights," according to Depczynski, "we terrified a lot of people. I remember one girl—her brother was Wally, we called him Beaver—when she saw us walking down the street she would go over to the other side." Depczynski's mother served as treasurer.[45]

The leader of a subcultural youth movement and yet immersed in a commodified ethnicity, Depczynski personifies what Raymond Williams has termed "emergent" culture (forms having to do with work of new kinds) and "residual" culture (forms having to do with work made in different societies, yet still available). More than that, he exemplifies a certain definition of culture: culture as dynamic process, as transition between past and present, as the accommodation of contradictions, as a curious amalgam of rebellion and conformity, whether within one person, a subculture, or a culture of youth.[46]

In an age horrified by certain kinds of ideological expressions, Buffalo's public officials may well have identified the Black Ts as a threatening mass movement, reminiscent, perhaps, of Mussolini's Fasci di Combatimento, paramilitary combat squads known familiarly as the Black Shirts. Or perhaps, as newspaper accounts suggest, the police only wished to head off an anticipated gang war. For whatever reason, the Black Ts found themselves under attack. In late August 1955, the police, having learned of an impending clash between two gangs in the Broadway-Fillmore area, identified the Black Ts as one of the gangs. "We keep a watchful eye on these boys with the black shirts, ducktail haircuts and zoot-suits," police captain John Tutuska said at the time, "because they're usually up to no good." That evening precinct police barred a dozen Black Ts from a Sears Street dance (as Depczynski recalls, "they barred me from my own street dance"). Depczynski's mother claimed that the police action made the youths "look like hoodlums." In addition, police may have banned the sale or wearing of black T-shirts. According to one account, the police announced that anyone wearing a black T-shirt would be arrested; according to another, Mayor Frank Sedita banned the sale of black T-shirts ("you couldn't buy a black T-shirt in Buffalo"). Tutuska disputes both recollections: "They certainly were not banned . . . no way that could have happened."[47]

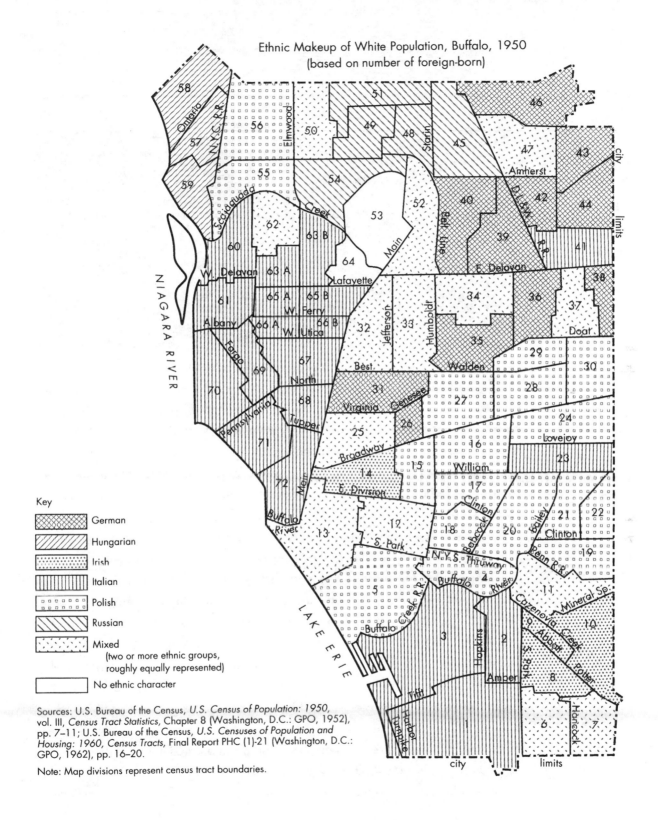

Ethnic Makeup of White Population, Buffalo, 1950
(based on number of foreign-born)

Key

German	
Hungarian	
Irish	
Italian	
Polish	
Russian	
Mixed	(two or more ethnic groups, roughly equally represented)
No ethnic character	

Sources: U.S. Bureau of the Census, *U.S. Census of Population: 1950,*
vol. III, *Census Tract Statistics*, Chapter 8 (Washington, D.C.: GPO, 1952),
pp. 7–11; U.S. Bureau of the Census, *U.S. Censuses of Population and
Housing: 1960, Census Tracts*, Final Report PHC (1)-21 (Washington, D.C.:
GPO, 1962), pp. 16–20.

Note: Map divisions represent census tract boundaries.

Hazing of pledges at Tau Zeta Tau, c. 1953. Although the media often focused on and sensationalized such rituals, many opponents of the secret societies were more concerned with their independence from school authority. Courtesy, Angelo Coniglio and Tau Zeta Tau.

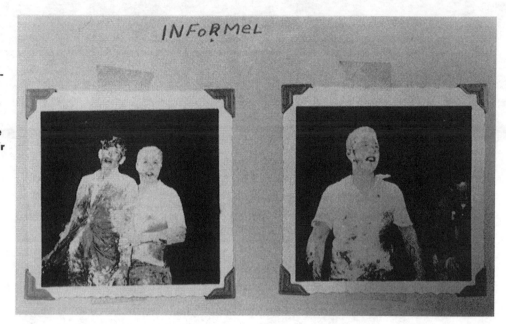

The Buffalo area also had a well-developed system of high school fraternities and sororities. The "secret societies," as they were sometimes called, were entrenched at Bennett, Lafayette, Grover Cleveland, Fosdick-Masten Park, and other inner-city public, nonvocational high schools, and in some suburbs, including Kenmore. In 1950, many of these organizations were decades old and rich in tradition.[48] Like the gangs, fraternities and sororities encouraged group identity and gave the group a public presence with items of personal paraphernalia: a ring, a sweatshirt, a jacket, or an insignia (emblazoned on the jacket or used to advertise the society in the back pages of the school yearbook).

The societies secured new members through annual rounds of rushing, pledging, and initiation. The sorority rush party was likely to be an elegant, finger-sandwich affair ("my first chicken salad," recalls one woman). Once pledged, aspirants to membership, male and female, were put through a one- to six-week hazing period. (Hazing is essentially a rite of passage, in which neophytes seeking the high status of membership enter a state of "liminality," described by anthropologist Victor Turner as an ambiguous and arbitrary statusless limbo "that has few or none of the attributes of the past or coming state" and whose function it is to prepare prospective members to accept the values and norms of the community or group.) Fraternal hazing was often physical. In Lafayette's Tau Zeta Tau, for example, pledge "slaves" who failed to satisfy member "masters" received

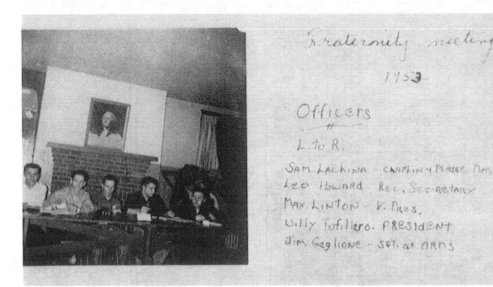

A formal meeting of Tau Zeta Tau, held at the Butler Mitchell Boys Club, 1953. Washington's portrait, although only incidentally captured in this photograph, reflects the organization's investment in the values of the dominant culture. Courtesy, Angelo Coniglio and Tau Zeta Tau.

demerits and ultimately a sound paddling at the weekly meeting. At Tri Gamma Phi, a sorority based at Mount St. Mary's, pledges were required to fill an entire roll of adhesive tape with pennies.[49] Both fraternities and sororities liked to use "Hell Night" or initiation to cover the bodies of pledges with foreign matter, such as eggs and flour or feathers and glue. Another typical practice by both sororities and fraternities was a week's rental of a summer beach cottage, a custom known as "Cottage Week."

There is ample evidence, however, of more obvious seriousness of purpose. Meetings of Tau Zeta Tau, for example, began with the pledge of allegiance, followed Roberts' *Rules of Order*, and ended with group prayer. Alpha Theta Sigma, a Kenmore sorority, required obedience to written rules of social conduct. It was also common for each society to sponsor its own elaborate, annual, off-campus dance. Alpha Theta Sigma sorority was identified with the "Autumn Leaves" dance (leaf-shaped dance programs), while Lafayette's Tau Zeta Tau was known for its Valentine's Day function (heart-shaped programs).[50]

In Buffalo, fraternities and sororities were organized by ethnic group, neighborhood, socioeconomic class, race, and religion—categories that not only clashed at the time with the public schools' thrust toward homogeneity but in our day again raise the issue of the appropriateness of the term "youth culture." At Bennett High, the secret societies were either Protestant, Catholic, or Jewish. Fosdick-Masten Park had a Jewish sorority. The religious distinction at Bennett, a college-preparatory institution in the 1940s and 1950s, was in part a class dis-

A typical practice by both sororities and fraternities was a week's rental of a summer beach cottage, a custom known as "Cottage Week." Courtesy, Angelo Coniglio and Tau Zeta Tau.

tinction, since the Jewish students, organized in Sigma Chi, were also the school's economic elite, while the Catholic students, members of Alpha Zeta, came from working-class families. Buffalo's rich ethnic heritage and strong neighborhoods also encouraged selection by ethnicity. Tau Zeta Tau's "macho young Italian-Americans," with names such as Montagino, Croglio, Zabaldo, and Donatelli, now and then got together with the "European Apple Pickers" of Sigma Alpha Rho, who were also Italian. Lafayette's Sigma Psi was largely an Irish group.

PRIVATE SPACE

The fraternities and sororities were also part of a larger search for a scarce postwar commodity: private space. If these organizations had a public face, they were also "secret," physically and spiritually detached from the schools, recreation programs, and other institutions of the dominant culture. A certain kind of private space—where, according to Herbert Marcuse, "man may become and remain 'himself,' "—could also be had in the darkened recesses of neighborhood movie theaters, in the back room of the Tropical Inn on Military Road, at the beach or in amusement parks, on the *Canadiana*, or in the soda shops, record stores, and restaurants that catered to youth. The autonomy of private space was also made accessible by the automobile, bicycle, or motorcycle. And the great majority of postwar Buffalo teenagers achieved physical autonomy by just putting one foot in front of the other: "we walked," one woman recalls; "you walked everywhere."[51]

School presented enormous obstacles to privacy and autonomy, but even there, there was one place—the bathroom—where students could risk a cigarette or engage in other officially forbidden activities. Cartoons in school yearbooks reveal the cafeteria as a sharply contested (though scarcely private) space, claimed by both students and administrators. Also, posted regulations forbidding students from leaving the cafeteria before the end of the lunch period suggest official anxiety over how students might spend genuinely "free" time. If all else failed, a young person could find autonomy by disaffiliating—either from the school, as a dropout, or from society, as a beatnik or a "beat."[52]

Buffalo youths from every social class shared this desire for the autonomy of organization and private space, just as they shared the centrality of music, dress, style, and other aspects of a culture built on consumption and leisure. As the success of "Hound Dog" Lorenz attests, some black and white youths— the cutting edge of youth culture, if you will—were bound by similar musical preferences. Yet when teenagers organized clubs or spent money on recreation, the preferences of "youth" proved an insufficient guide to conduct. At this point, class, race, ethnicity, neighborhood, and gender came to the fore as critical categories of understanding, perception, and action.

Slumber-party antics, 1956. Cy Gamma Cy (their spelling) was a junior high sorority in Kenmore, New York, a close-in suburb of Buffalo. Stanley Aronowitz explains the slumber party as a "ritual of autonomy because it requires that the parents understand that they are not to interfere with the girls' time together" (*False Promises*, p. 83). Courtesy, Virginia Kelley.

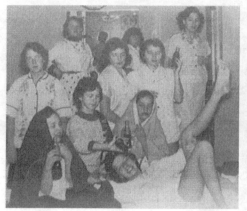 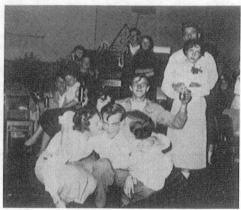

Underage drinking was commonplace in the Buffalo area in the mid-1950s. At the Tropical Inn on Military Road, Kenmore girls partied with boys from other communities. "One night they raided the place and took some of the girls downtown." C. 1953. Courtesy, Gail Whitman.

Schine's Riverside Theater, Tonawanda Street, c. 1940. Courtesy, *Riverside Review*.

The proverbial
back seat. C. 1953.
Courtesy, Angelo
Coniglio.

In an institution characterized by intensive observation, high school restrooms offered opportunities for unsupervised peer-group interaction. Grover Cleveland, *Clevelander*, 1952.

Cartoon by Mussen, Buffalo Technical, *Techtonian*, 1951.

At Girls Vocational, student monitors were charged with enforcing a posted regulation against meandering students. *Herald*, 1948.

Bishop Timon seniors, enjoying their smoking privilege in the school cafeteria. *Talisman*, 1962. The Surgeon General's report, linking cigarette smoking to lung cancer, was issued in January 1964.

John Bray (*left*), pictured here with David Holdsworth in 1959, was one of the few Buffalo teenagers who might be described as "beat." A boatneck shirt of the type worn by Bray had appeared on the cover of Jack Kerouac's *On the Road*, the beat novel first published in 1957. Courtesy, David Holdsworth.

SUBCULTURE

Young pianist Brennan Jacques was a figment of the USIA's hegemonic imagination—no more a typical teenager than television's Nelsons were a typical family. Behind the idealized image of a somewhat rebellious but blessedly homogeneous youth culture was a richer and, for some, more threatening social reality founded on distinct subcultures.

Despite a variety of shared experiences, the sexes inhabited separate and different youth subcultures. Boys' subculture was a subculture of the street, aggressive and dramatic. Girls' subculture was more likely to be an indoor variety, intimate rather than aggressive, playful rather than dramatic (although the existence of girl gangs and their role in the *Canadiana* riot suggest that girls' culture was shaped by variables of class and race and that scholars have overdrawn the image of passive interiority). Boys' subculture was captured by the blood rituals of Buffalo gangs and by the custom of street-corner lounging. Girls' subculture more often meant playing cards with older women; romantic, distanced attachments to movie stars and pop singers built around pasting pictures in a scrapbook or collecting "Ponytail" accessories, pins, charms, or other objects; studying on the living room floor, surrounded by phone, record player, books, a Coke—and other girls; and the slumber party, an institution defined by a shared physical intimacy, including the ubiquitous collapsing human pyramid. In an era marked by anxiety over masculinity and extraordinarily hostile to expressions of male homosexuality, boys' subculture found expression in the cult of the automobile, the wrestling mania of the late 1950s, school athletics, and other examples of the "American tough." Girls, in contrast, felt free to touch each other tenderly, to publicly demonstrate intimacy by wearing identical clothing, and to dance with each other.[53]

Social class was of overriding importance in determining style, clothing, music preference, and other characteristics of youth subculture. Even sexuality, or more properly attitudes toward sexuality, was a function of class. We know from the Kinsey reports, published in 1948 and 1953, that working-class youth had more sex, and had it earlier, than middle-class youth. Photographs reveal nothing so private as sexual conduct, but they do suggest differences in attitude. Yearbook photographs—what looks like a mockup of a soda bar, from the 1953 Bishop

Dan, with the top down. 1952. Courtesy, Gail Whitman.

Mike Sendlbeck, shown here in about 1953 with his bored, ported, relieved, and stroked sportsman-class stock car, started racing at age fourteen (when the legal age was eighteen) and at fifteen had opened his own hop-up shop at 1246 Genesee. "I was what you called a motor-head when I was a kid. Cars always thrilled me." This photo was taken in the pits at Civic Stadium. Courtesy, Mike Sendlbeck.

Bo and Ron perfect the skill of leaning on an object lower than one's elbow, 1953. *Left:* Bo's '46 Mercury. *Right:* Ron's '50 Ford. Courtesy, Jerry Szefel.

Boys touching, 1950. Courtesy, Angelo Coniglio.

Mothers and daughters playing cards on Southampton Street, 1953. Courtesy, Gretchen Martin.

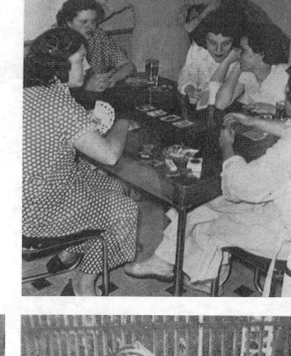

Bennett students studying. *Beacon*, commencement issue, 1959. Girls were often photographed on the floor and engaged in multiple activities. No similar photographs of boys exist, and boys were seldom, if ever, photographed while studying.

Girls touching, 1954. Bennett *Beacon*, Christmas issue.

Slumber-party pyramid, Alpha Theta Sigma sorority, Kenmore, c. 1959. Courtesy, Virginia Kelley.

Timon yearbook; two teens sharing a 7-Up at a YMCA snack bar in 1957; some Bennett students at a local soda shop, also in 1957; and two Bennett seniors, outfitted in saddle shoes, sharing a stairway—as a group suggest an overview of what middle-class sexuality was or was supposed to be: dreamy, fraternal, mediated by commodities. In sharp contrast, photographs of working-class girls reveal a more aggressive attitude toward sexuality and what would seem to be an almost brazen openness to experience. As Mica Nava has written, girls lacked some of the protest options open to boys and were therefore likely to use sexuality as a form of rebellion, with consequences at once predictable and unfortunate. Aggressive sexual conduct might constitute a challenge to school and parents, but through intercourse, pregnancy, and motherhood, it also bound girls even more completely to dependency on boys and to traditional notions of the feminine.[54]

One of the best examples of the centrality of class involves the combination of pink and black colors now linked in the collective imagination with both the 1950s and teenagers. When this color combination emerged in the early 1950s, it bore no relation to the "Happy Days" mythology it now evokes. Pink and black were in this first incarnation clearly countercultural, bound first to black culture and then to southern, working-class rockabilly music, signifying opposition to the authority of the dominant culture. And why pink and black? Two reasons. First, because they so obviously did not belong together: pink was the color of innocent girlish domesticity, black the embodiment of male malevolence. To put the two side by side was to "marry" pink and black, with all that implied. Second, pink and black were not the colors of authority. There were no school athletic teams decked out in pink and black, nor was there a single national flag that combined these colors. In the terminology of color description, neither pink nor black was a primary color, and hence the combination was ideally suited to represent the "secondary" working class. Of course, it did not take long for the dominant culture to begin exploiting the color combination for its own purposes. By 1954, pink and black were being used by home decorators in bathrooms and kitchens, and in advertising for laundry detergent and Coca-Cola. And in 1955, pink and black were the featured colors at an American Legion fashion show in Buffalo. Only by shedding the link to black and working-class ideology could the pink-and-black combination come finally (and spuriously) to represent the larger entity of youth culture.[55]

The experience of coming of age in Buffalo was very much a product of where one lived—of geographical subculture, or neighborhood. The importance

of neighborhood may be illustrated by focusing on the way a particular neighborhood shaped the lives of the youths who grew up within its spatial, cultural, and chronological boundaries. The area selected—centered at Masten and Southampton Streets in the Cold Spring area—was chosen because former residents of the neighborhood have remained in contact. The last reunion of the old neighborhood, held in 1984, drew about 125 people, some from as far away as Arizona.

In the late 1940s and early 1950s, the residential neighborhood around the intersection of Masten and Southampton Streets was white, German and Irish in ethnic content, and working class. Parents were steelworkers, printers, truck drivers, plumbers, and the like, and many of the young men who were teenagers in the early 1950s would soon find their way into the military and the Bethlehem mills. Neighborhood girls often quit high school at sixteen and, like their mothers, had few ambitions short of "getting married and having kids," one woman remembers. "Girls didn't think a lot about careers then." Housing was simple and comfortable enough. Most of the people in the neighborhood, that

Dreamy, middle-class sexuality at a soda bar near Bennett High School. Bennett *Beacon*, commencement issue, 1957.

In some middle-class institutions, an almost androgynous "student" culture appeared, in which boys and girls with similar aspirations resembled each other in style and appearance. Bennett *Beacon*, commencement issue, 1957.

*Working-class
Sexuality.*

**Working-class girls
at a Utica Street bar
in 1950–51. Cour-
tesy, Gail Whitman.**

An East Side couple, 1951–52. Courtesy, Jerry Szefel.

Sal and Me, 1955. Courtesy, Gail Whitman.

The Masten/South-ampton neighbor-hood as it appeared in 1984, looking north up Masten Street from the ele-vated playground at Masten and Dodge.

same woman adds, "had linoleum in their front rooms with a rug on top of it—and thought it was great."[56]

As we have seen, the youth culture of the 1950s was a leisure culture. The Masten/Southampton neighborhood had three centers of leisure activity. The first was at the heart of the residential neighborhood, at the corner of Masten and Southampton Streets. There, on summer evenings, neighborhood youths assembled in front of Kleinmeier's delicatessen, only to be moved off the corner by police or doused with water by an irritated upstairs tenant. Across the street, created in response to this harassment, was a short-lived soda bar, owned and operated by Rosanna Petrelli, eighteen, and her sister Marie, twenty-three. Although the soda bar was open only one year, in 1952–53, it is remembered for its jukebox, booths, and a special ice cream dish, the "Boomer Delight," named in honor of a local teenager.[57]

The second center of teenage activity was a long block to the south and east, encompassing the Masten Playground and the Civic Stadium. The playground is best remembered as the site of regular and intense handball games, played against the concrete backstops for small sums of money and often involving boy-girl teams. "You had to be good to play for money," recalls one woman. "And I was good." Civic Stadium was for older or more adventurous teens—gang members, or those ready for some recreational drinking or a game of craps under the stadium lights ("a nice girl did not go up there at night"). At one time or another, nearly every neighborhood youth sneaked into the stadium for the stock car races. At the stadium or the playground, smoking was widespread. A nickel chipped into the pot bought five Lucky Strikes.[58]

The third center of activity, within walking distance of Masten and Southampton, was the corner of Main and Utica Streets. There, within a few hundred yards, were Hi-Teen's Delwood Ballroom, Skateland (at the site of what is now McDonald's), and a variety of lesser attractions, including New Chicago Lunch, Your Host, the Deco restaurant, the Royal Arms night club, a bowling alley, and a pool room. Skating was the real passion, occupying Wednesday, Friday, and Sunday nights. Because of its many attractions for youth, the corner at Main and Utica also served as a point of contact between youth from different city neighborhoods and the close-in suburbs. As a gathering place, it was similar in function to the modern suburban mall. One important difference is that the mall was designed largely for adult shopping, and its appropriation by teenagers as a recreational space has been an informal process. The Main/Utica area, on the other hand, was pieced together by public agencies and private businesses primarily as a center for youth recreation. It stands as a good example of a kind of inner-city, public recreation that would soon disappear, its place taken not only by the suburban shopping mall but by the privatized leisure of the living room television set.[59]

The Masten/Southampton neighborhood changed dramatically in the mid-1950s as a result of large-scale population movements. Many white families left the city altogether, drawn to the suburbs by the promise of a trouble-free, homogeneous community and federal housing policies that subsidized suburban home ownership. At the same time, Buffalo's black population, driven northward by the razing of central city "ghetto" neighborhoods for urban renewal and attracted by housing vacated by suburban-bound whites, began to settle in Masten/Southampton. In Buffalo and other cities, these migrations were first experienced

A collection of wallet items from 1952–1954, as they appear in Gail Whitman's scrapbook. *Center:* Boomer, Betty, Gail, Jackie, Bill, and Ginger, with the Masten Park pool and Civic Stadium in the background. Courtesy, Gail Whitman.

In the 1950s, these courts were the site of regular handball games, played for small sums of money and often involving boy-girl teams. 1984.

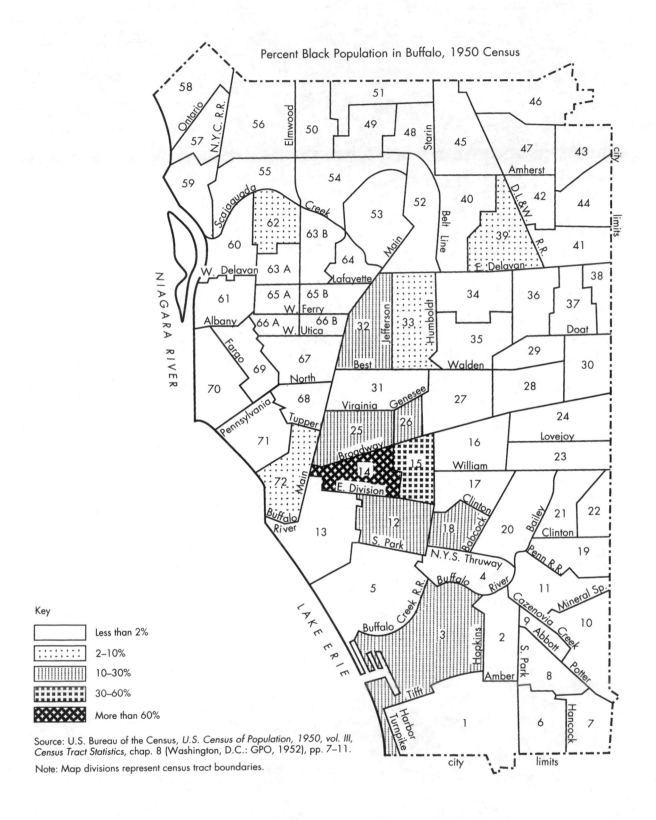

Percent Black Population in Buffalo, 1950 Census

Key

☐	Less than 2%
⣿ (dotted)	2–10%
▦ (vertical lines)	10–30%
▨ (hatched)	30–60%
▦ (cross-hatch)	More than 60%

Source: U.S. Bureau of the Census, *U.S. Census of Population, 1950, vol. III, Census Tract Statistics*, chap. 8 (Washington, D.C.: GPO, 1952), pp. 7–11.

Note: Map divisions represent census tract boundaries.

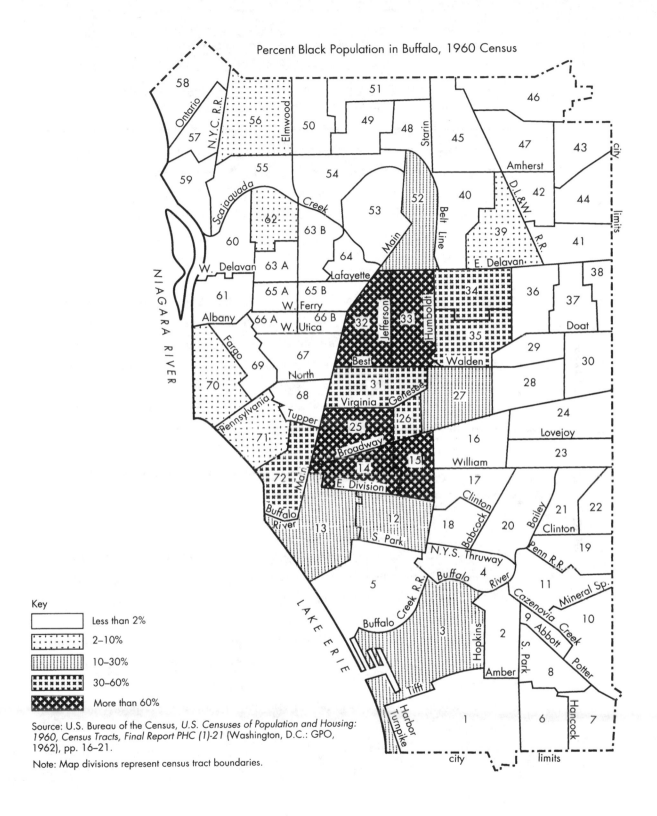

Percent Black Population in Buffalo, 1960 Census

Key

	Less than 2%
	2–10%
	10–30%
	30–60%
	More than 60%

Source: U.S. Bureau of the Census, *U.S. Censuses of Population and Housing: 1960, Census Tracts, Final Report PHC (1)-21* (Washington, D.C.: GPO, 1962), pp. 16–21.

Note: Map divisions represent census tract boundaries.

as tension and conflict between mobile teenagers, often over territory or "turf," as traditional boundaries between neighborhoods, ethnic groups, and races became increasingly problematic and indeterminate.[60] Although race was not at issue in the September 1953 fight between the Gunners and the Park Gang, that episode seems to have been one of the earliest of a series of incidents involving whites and blacks in and around the Masten/Southampton neighborhood. Doors once left open at all hours were now locked. In 1953, the neighborhood was white except for one or two families that were accepted in the area; by 1957, most white families had left the neighborhood for the suburbs or other parts of the city. By 1958, the Civic Stadium area was the scene of considerable violence among rival black gangs.[61]

The neighborhood girls were more likely to be affected by race than the boys, and for a good reason. Most of the boys attended Boys Vocational, Burgard, or other city vocational institutions with only a few black students. Many girls, on the other hand, attended Fosdick-Masten Park High School, a nearby, integrated, academic high school. When, despite petitioning and picketing by neighborhood youth and other residents, Fosdick-Masten Park was closed as an *academic* school in 1953, most of the neighborhood girls went on to nearby East High, where they again encountered a formally racially integrated environment and again experienced some difficulties. By the mid-1950s, physical encounters in which girls of one race were struck and knocked down by girls of another were a part of life in the neighborhood.[62]

Two aspects of the Masten-Southampton experience stand out. First, this neighborhood provided its teenage residents with several spaces that were sufficiently private to offer significant degrees of autonomy. One was Petrelli's soda bar, perhaps a unique example of teenage and young-adult efforts to create space for the young within the system of capitalism. Another was the stadium, where neighborhood youth had more to fear from the police than from parents.

Second, the experience of Masten-Southampton teenagers was primarily a local experience, in which activities were generated and organizations established within a limited geographical framework. Although some youths ventured out of the immediate area to attend Hi-Teen or go roller skating, it was for the most part the neighborhood that remained the locus for vital and lasting relationships, and it is the neighborhood around which regular reunions are still held. This local and particularistic perspective, made possible by the high concentrations of youths in the central city and perhaps reinforced and intensified by racial conflict, served as a barrier to the larger youth culture shaped by the medium of television and characterized by more universal experience.

Although Masten-Southampton teenagers would have recognized themselves as existing within a general youth culture encompassing certain organizational and stylistic dimensions, their spirit looked inward, toward the neighborhood and its particularities, rather than outward, toward other neighborhoods and other youths. In this sense, the history of Masten-Southampton exemplifies the centrality of subcultural experience for Buffalo youth.

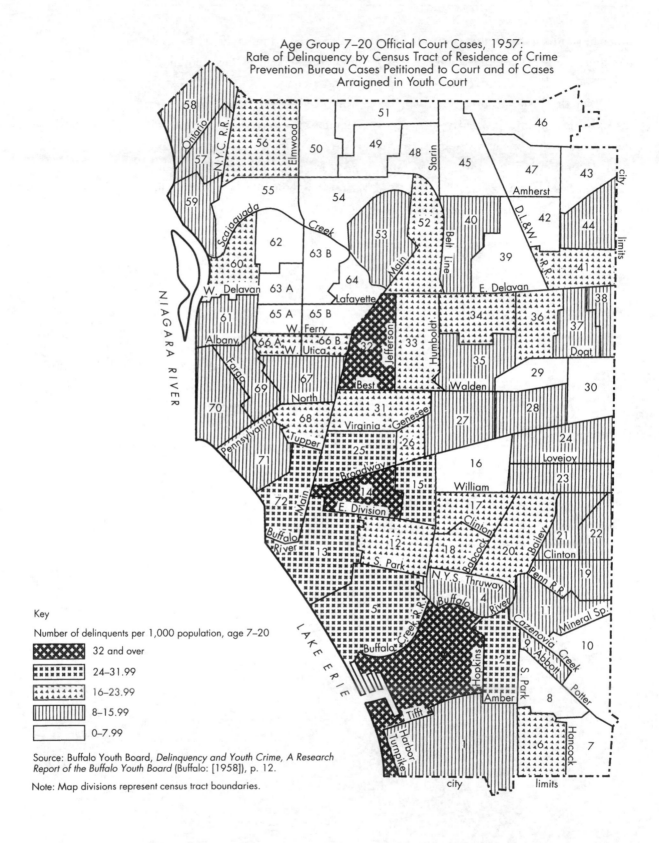

Age Group 7–20 Official Court Cases, 1957:
Rate of Delinquency by Census Tract of Residence of Crime
Prevention Bureau Cases Petitioned to Court and of Cases
Arraigned in Youth Court

Key

Number of delinquents per 1,000 population, age 7–20

- 32 and over
- 24–31.99
- 16–23.99
- 8–15.99
- 0–7.99

Source: Buffalo Youth Board, *Delinquency and Youth Crime, A Research Report of the Buffalo Youth Board* (Buffalo: [1958]), p. 12.

Note: Map divisions represent census tract boundaries.

S O C I A L

E N G I N E E R I N G

J U V E N I L E   D E L I N Q U E N C Y

In 1951, Buffalo Children's Court Judge Victor Wylegala, in language evocative of the era's anti-Communist ethos, warned the people of western New York to guard against complacency. "We are entering a critical period," he wrote, "a period which could bring disaster to the community's young people." The source of Wylegala's concern was not the Red Tide, but what the popular magistrate feared would be a new wave of juvenile delinquency as bad as that experienced during World War II—or worse. As a predictor of the future, Wylegala was remarkably astute. Youth arrests increased substantially in 1953 (the year of the Gunner/Park Gang rumble) and by the late 1950s delinquency rates in Buffalo were approaching the relatively high levels of the mid-1940s. Although the mania over delinquency also proved useful to those seeking a return to prewar gender roles—working mothers were described as "losing [the war] on the home front"—the problem was real enough.[63]

Wylegala was most concerned with a subculture of delinquent youth, but he was not alone in wondering if middle-class youth had not also become vulnerable to the allure of social rebellion. The doubts that many parents and public officials had about the middle class were reflected in an article that appeared in the suburban *Amherst Bee* in 1957. Titled "Most Teen-agers Are Good, and Eggertsville Woman Will Vouch for It," it told the story of two YMCA-affiliated boys, both devoted to their "hot rod" cars, who had stopped to help a woman change a tire. Another example: Evidence that the YMCA Junior Leaders Club was doing cleanup duty three times a week at the Delaware Avenue branch led the group's eighteen-year-old adviser to say, "It goes a long way to defeat any idea that all kids are hoodlums."[64]

The point is that some adults believed that all kids were hoodlums, and many adults believed that all kids were *potential* hoodlums. While juvenile delinquency had heretofore seemed thoroughly isolated within working-class subculture, changing social conditions raised legitimate fears that delinquent behavior was percolating up through the social structure. At the center of the problem was a new and heterogeneous school population. Quite simply, the high schools were overflowing with all kinds of youths—black, the working class, second-generation immigrants—who had in the past gone directly from grade school to the workplace. Instead, they were now in the schools, rubbing shoulders, exchanging notes, and sharing their lives and subcultures with the white middle class that had always been there. Much the same thing was happening at the Zanzibar Lounge, on the *Canadiana*, and at the corner of Main and Utica. But the schools were a special kind of social pressure cooker, and it was there that most attention was concentrated.

Two very different social-engineering approaches to the problem of delinquency emerged. The first approach was to attempt to change the behavior of delinquents or incipient delinquents. In this category fall the city's efforts to restrict unsupervised activity such as corner lounging, and to replace it with organized, adult-supervised recreation; attacks on the mass media; the Dress Right campaign; the Working Boys Home; and the Catholic Church's efforts at moral exhortation.

The second approach accepted delinquency as a subcultural given, and sought to erect barriers between "delinquent" subcultures and middle-class youth, defined as vulnerable. Bob Wells's Hi-Teen, which used a dress code to restrict the access of working-class youth, was one such effort. Another, much more important, was the city's system of vocational schools. Finally, school officials erected ideological barriers between social classes, sending one set of messages to working-class youth, another to middle-class youth.

Buffalo's war against juvenile delinquency was waged on many fronts. From his Children's Court bench, Wylegala sent vandals and other youthful offenders off to "reform school," though not often enough to satisfy a citizenry increasingly critical of the judge's reputation for permissiveness. Like many other newspapers across the country, the *Courier-Express* entertained its readers with a series of cartoons on delinquency, usually representing civic authorities cowering before armed thugs.[65] The Buffalo Youth Board, created in late 1955 as the city's official weapon against juvenile delinquency, gathered an impressive array of statistics, including some linking high delinquency rates to particular areas of the city. The Youth Board also produced a 1956 film, *Car Theft*, dealing with one of the few delinquent acts identified with middle-class youth, and 50,000 copies of "The Chicken Pamphlet," an effort to turn youth away from blood rituals and other adolescent rites of initiation and tests of courage and loyalty practiced by local gangs.[66]

In the fall of 1953, Buffalo police and magistrates began to enforce a city ordinance against "corner lounging," a relatively innocuous if irritating activity believed to have some relationship to more advanced forms of delinquent behavior. Police made arrests at Cazenovia and Seneca, French and Fillmore, Broadway and Madison, in the 2600 block of Main Street, and at Louisiana Street and South Park Avenue, where, according to one police officer, a "goon squad" of eight to ten teenagers had been blocking the sidewalk. Youth who took to the corners following the 9:00 P.M. closing of the Babcock Boys Club were labeled "candy-kitchen cake-eaters" by Captain McNamara of the Babcock precinct. "Bring some of these adolescent apes into the station and don't treat them gently," suggested McNamara. "These punks have more respect for a cop's night stick than for the entire Code of Criminal Procedure."[67]

Taken in isolation, the campaign against corner lounging appears frivolous. It can best be appreciated as part of a larger and exceedingly influential explanation for juvenile delinquency that emphasized the dearth of supervised recreational facilities. According to this view, delinquent behavior occurred almost inadvertently, as a result of youth's misuse of its overabundant leisure. Full of energy and lacking either strong parental guidance or "wholesome" recreational outlets, youths fell under the influence of a thoughtless and irresponsible peer group and into delinquent patterns of street-corner lounging, vandalism, car theft, and gang formation. While not unreasonable, this "recreation" argument denied to delinquency any social content or purpose; by implication, youths vandalized schools and cemeteries because there was nothing else to do.[68]

Nevertheless, enormous energy and resources were devoted to supervised youth recreation. Besides regular church and school programs, in 1950 the city had at least thirty-five recreation centers, ten under public control, the remainder operated by the YMCA and YWCA, the Boys Clubs, the Salvation Army, the Buffalo Urban League (in the Ellicott district), and the Neighborhood House Association (in the Masten district). Several new facilities were constructed or opened in the 1950s, including the Masten Boys Club at 72 Kingsley (later cred-

Renovating a spring at the Youth Opportunity Camp, Great Valley, New York, August 1964. This camp—essentially a reform school—was for boys "on the threshold of delinquency." The *Courier-Express* Collection of the Buffalo and Erie County Historical Society and E. H. Butler Library at State University College at Buffalo. All rights reserved.

Leo Joseph Roche, Buffalo *Courier-Express*, 1956. A reflection of the helplessness many adults felt over the problem of juvenile delinquency. The *Courier-Express* Collection of the Buffalo and Erie County Historical Society and E. H. Butler Library at State University College at Buffalo. All rights reserved.

A scene from *Car Theft*, a film produced for the Buffalo Youth Board in 1956. Buffalo Youth Board, *Report*, 1957. "The street corner," said the *Report*, "may become the rendezvous where amateur criminals plan an act of petty car theft."

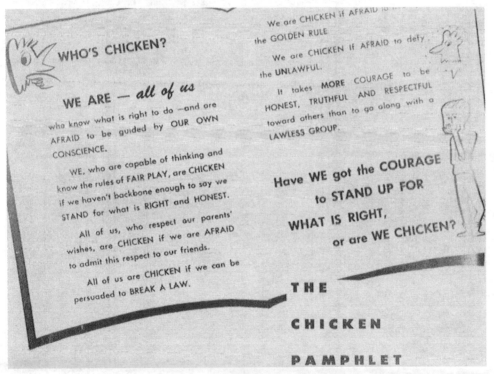

WHO'S CHICKEN?

WE ARE — *all of us*

who know what is right to do —and are AFRAID to be guided by OUR OWN CONSCIENCE.

WE, who are capable of thinking and know the rules of FAIR PLAY, are CHICKEN if we haven't backbone enough to say we STAND for what is RIGHT and HONEST.

All of us, who respect our parents' wishes, are CHICKEN if we are AFRAID to admit this respect to our friends.

All of us are CHICKEN if we can be persuaded to BREAK A LAW.

We are CHICKEN if AFRAID to [...] the GOLDEN RULE

We are CHICKEN IF AFRAID to defy the UNLAWFUL.

It takes MORE COURAGE to be HONEST, TRUTHFUL AND RESPECTFUL toward others than to go along with a LAWLESS GROUP.

Have WE got the COURAGE to STAND UP FOR WHAT IS RIGHT, or are WE CHICKEN?

THE CHICKEN PAMPHLET

Text from "The Chicken Pamphlet," written for the Buffalo Youth Board c. 1956. Buffalo Youth Board, *Report*, 1957. The pamphlet was a response to reports that West Side gangs were administering "courage" tests, in which youth who cried out in pain when cut with a knife on the back of the hand were labeled "chicken" and denied gang membership.

Hanging around near the Babcock Boys Club, c. 1950. This sort of aimless activity was thought to be a stepping stone to real delinquency. Courtesy, Paul Missana and the Buffalo Boys Clubs.

Outside the Butler-Mitchell Boys Club, Massachusetts Avenue, August 1962. Original caption: "TIME ON THEIR HANDS—That's one of the biggest problems facing school dropouts. They have no money, no jobs, nothing to do except 'hang around' as dramatized here in a picture posed by members of the Butler Mitchell Club." They had trouble looking bad. Courtesy, Paul Missana and the Buffalo Boys Clubs.

This back page of a YMCA pamphlet embodied the organization's faith in recreation as a cure for delinquency. C. 1940. Courtesy, YMCA of the USA and the Delaware YMCA, Buffalo.

"We were a family. We were drawn down there. You had to be there." Taken at Poli's Shoe Store, Fillmore and Landon, 1953. Courtesy, Robert Bryce.

ited with having kept club members out of the 1953 gang wars) and a Youth Board lounge in the Cold Spring area. The YMCA opened an interracial Teen Canteen (the name taken from World War II USO facilities) on Michigan Avenue and was especially active in the suburbs, opening teen centers, snack bars, or "Y Teen Towns" in Kenmore, Orchard Park, Cheektowaga, Tonawanda, and Maryvale in the late 1950s and early 1960s. Some clubs, including the interracial "Teen Towners" in the Riverside section of the city, were created independently of the YMCA or any other formal organization.[69] Although most of these programs granted participating youth some role in governance, their purpose was to encourage teenagers to spend their leisure time indoors, in a generally public setting, and under adult supervision.

Recreation was also the preferred solution within the city's small but determined middle-class black community. By the late 1940s, black youth had access to a variety of youth organizations, including Gamma Girls, Kappa Rho, Cold Spring Boys, Dukes Club, Theta Club, and Fri-Y Youth Den. The voice of the black community, the *Buffalo Criterion*, applauded the entry of the municipal government into youth recreation in 1945 and described the city council's 1951 closing of thirty-four playgrounds as a "municipal tragedy." In an approach unique to the black community and anticipating the Moynihan Report on the black family, the *Criterion* called on the community's "men" to become "actively interested in our children" if delinquency were to be prevented.[70]

A hard-line, old-fashioned approach to delinquency was apparent at the Working Boys Home at 4 Vermont Street, known as "Boys' Town of the East," where the "fighting priest," Monsignor Franklin Kelliher, had been battling juvenile delinquency and youth culture and "saving" the city's most hardened youth since the mid-1930s. For Kelliher, corner lounging, rock 'n' roll, fraternities and sororities, gangs, metal-studded belts, and youth crime were all symptoms of a "rising, engulfing wave of adolescent lawlessness" on the city's West Side and throughout Erie County. In 1957, Kelliher had delivered an impromptu lecture and sermon behind the Niagara police station before eight "hoodlums" who had attacked two Boys Home residents. "Too many of our youths," he said, "are more interested in sex than sports. They're interested in hot-rods and hound dogs, and you wouldn't want to hear what I think of Elvis Presley." The answer, he believed, was a return to more direct and more physical forms of authority. "If I must get tough with mad dogs and sadists to protect worthwhile lads," he said, "I will do it." A former amateur boxer who had wrestled professionally under the name of the

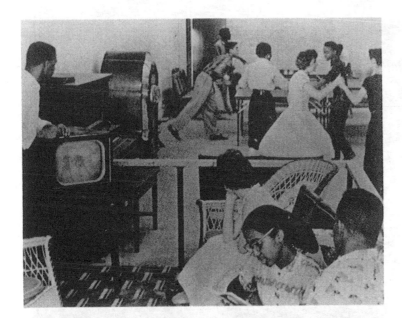

The teen lounge, like this possibly idealized version photographed for the 1957 Buffalo Youth Board *Report*, represented an effort to reach youth by offering them the media culture they valued—though under adult supervision.

Herbert Hoover, who in the 1950s was chairman of the board of the Boys Clubs of America, holding forth in the Babcock Club game room. Hoover saw the clubs as a counterweight to a mobile society that had cut away at the "moral restraints of community life." Courtesy, Paul Missana and the Buffalo Boys Clubs.

The Working Boys
Home, 4 Vermont
Street, before it
was replaced by a
new structure in the
early 1960s. Franklin
Kelliher Collection,
Courtesy Rev. Wal-
ter Kern, archivist,
Diocese of Buffalo.

"Masked Marvel," Kelliher promoted the local Golden Gloves tournament and used his pugilistic skills and physical presence to intimidate, and presumably win the respect of, the boys at the home. He liked to tell the story of how, in his third day on the job in 1936, he had thrown down the gauntlet to a group of boys who had refused to accept his authority. Presenting four sets of boxing gloves, Kelliher challenged the boys to fight him for control of the home: "If you lick me, I'll quit. If I lick you, you will take orders and obey." Within minutes, the six-foot, 235-pound priest had dispatched two boys and a third had pulled the gloves off. "I never had a boy who could beat me," Kelliher recalled, "nor any who could even warm me up."[71]

While Kelliher's enthusiasm for discipline no doubt appealed to many citizens, his methods of dealing with youth were not those of the main body of the Catholic Church. Created in 1941, the youth program of the diocese of western New York was by the early 1950s moving toward "progressive" methods pioneered by turn-of-the-century educators. In this vein, a diocesan youth council was created in 1949, and by the mid-1950s Catholic youth were voting as delegates at annual

Monsignor Kelliher's income as a professional wrestler helped finance the purchase of the Vermont Street building. Although his physical approach to the problem of discipline was increasingly seen as outmoded, it no doubt had considerable impact on youths in an age that revered toughness and still believed in the boxing ring as a place where the young could learn life's lessons and even—in the case of Rocky Graziano, for example—escape a life of crime. Franklin Kelliher Collection, Courtesy Rev. Walter Kern, archivist, Diocese of Buffalo.

diocesan youth conventions and working on parish publications where they were to develop "responsibility" and "fraternal feeling." When leaders from the Catholic Youth Council (CYC) "took over" city government in 1953, Buffalo's acting mayor Elmer F. Lux praised the CYC program as "a real threat" against "the Godless surge that threatens the entire world."[72]

The church was very much aware of the social needs of postwar youth. It sought at once to meet and contain those needs by sponsoring parish dances and, later, record hops. In North Buffalo, for example, the Friday-night parish dances, rotating among St. Margaret's, Holy Spirit, St. Vincent's, and other area churches, were the most important social events of the weekend, and not just for Catholics. "Back in those days," recalls an area resident, "the CYO (Catholic Youth Organization) was the big thing."[73]

Dancing in the church gymnasium, under the watchful eye of the priest, was one thing. More private activities, including necking and petting and "going steady," were another. Here the church could only "educate" and exhort, and it did plenty of both. Through the diocesan paper, the *Union and Echo*, youths were told that high school boys who approved of necking and petting had degraded themselves by taking on the "color of their environment." Going steady, arguably a reasonable practice among teenagers who would be marrying before age twenty, was found "stupid, silly, juvenile, nonsensical, time-wasting, class destroying, vitiating," and "dangerous." One solution was to keep sex-education films that "may be an occasion of sin" out of the public schools; another was to promote moral values through CYC courses on courtship and marriage. At bottom, moral torpor was a function of religious ignorance. "If God and His Teachings are unknown to a teenager," wrote one cleric, "what is there to . . . keep pure and unsullied the virgin purity of a girl friend because she is the prototype of the Virgin of Virgins—Mary?"[74]

If impiety was the fundamental cause of delinquency, the mass media—books, advertising, television, and especially movies—were not far behind. The church's Legion of Decency Ratings warned Catholics about *Bad Sister, Roadhouse, Anna Karenina*, and other films that might be "objectionable in part." In March 1955, thirteen features, including *They Were So Young*, were listed under the new category of "condemned" films. Although *Blackboard Jungle* was causing riots in movie theaters all over the world, its indictment of the public school system spared the film the lowest rating. The church hierarchy carefully monitored local screenings. When theaters continued to show condemned films, Catholics were asked to boycott the offending theater. A case of this kind occurred in 1955, over the showing of *Son of Sinbad* at the Twin Drive-In Theater at Walden and Dick Roads. Public authorities were less concerned with film than with the print media. The Mayor's Advisory Committee on Salacious Publications and the Buffalo Youth Board focused their attention on comic books, "girlie" magazines, and other materials that might incite youth to "lust and sex crimes."[75]

DRESS RIGHT

From police to school administrators, Buffalo public officials clearly believed that dress and behavior were closely linked and that delinquent behavior was related to extreme, bizarre, or sloppy dress and to such specific items of apparel as sweatshirts and T-shirts. In the mid-1950s, these beliefs led to Buffalo's best-known contribution to the campaign against juvenile delinquency: a dress code for the public schools, known as Dress Right.[76] Although the code was most obviously a rather primitive effort to change the behavior of delinquent youth by changing modes of dress, it also functioned in a variety of other, more sophisticated and interesting ways.

The Dress Right code was the brainchild of Joseph E. Manch, who as associate superintendent for pupil personnel services had observed the correlation between delinquency and dress during suspension hearings conducted under his office. Late in 1955, Manch moved to turn this correlation into a program of social action. But rather than impose a code from above, and risk its rejection as a manifestation of adult or administrative authority, Manch broached the idea of a dress code to the Inter-High [Student] Council. The Dress Right code developed by the council and cleared through Manch contained separate recommendations for boys and girls as well as for academic and vocational high schools, in effect reinforcing gender roles and, more important, delineating the class differences implicit in a school system that so clearly demarcated vocational and academic education.

A photograph from the 1958 Burgard Vocational yearbook shows a portion of the code displayed on a cafeteria wall. The last line of the poster—"White Bucks Acceptable"—implies that a debate had taken place over this particular item of apparel and reveals the extent to which clothing had become politicized.

In theory, student adherence to the code's recommendations was entirely vol-

The cafeteria at Burgard Vocational, with the Dress Right code on the wall. *Craftsman*, 1958. The photograph reveals a number of youths in violation of the code.

This Week
MAGAZINE

Herald NEW YORK *Tribune*

November 23, 1958

Buffalo's
Magic
Mirror

In theory, student adherence to the code was voluntary. To stimulate compliance, one school installed a full-length two-way mirror. A camera recorded students' reactions to their appearance and to a sign above the mirror, which asked, "Are you satisfied?" At Lafayette, coercion was the rule; boys who showed up without ties were sent home to get them.

untary. One institution hoped to stimulate compliance by installing a full-length mirror, inscribed with the words, "Look! This is you. Are *you* satisfied?" These and other persuasive techniques seem to have succeeded. At Fosdick-Masten Girls Vocational, the principal reported a dramatic change in student attire. "They used to come to exams in dungarees, but not any more," he said. Now there were "no pin curls, no dungarees, no slacks—all dresses." Many principals claimed the dress program had improved student behavior.

Manch's results and methods found a receptive national audience. Manch and Caesar Naples, student head of the Inter-High Council, went to Chicago to discuss the Dress Right program on CBS's "Good Morning Show," hosted by Will Rogers, Jr. The *New York Herald Tribune* and the *New York World-Telegram and Sun* carried well-illustrated features on the code, and *Newsweek* illustrated its

Photographs accompanying *Newsweek's* coverage of Dress Right, March 11, 1957, captured the prevailing view that clothes affected behavior. UPI.

Bejeaned girls behave better . . .

United Press Photos

. . . when they're in ladylike dress

coverage with two photographs, one of a "bejeaned" girl, the other of a better-behaved counterpart in "ladylike dress." Dress Right also received elaborate publicity through the American Institute of Men's and Boys' Wear, an apparel-industry trade association that must have relished the prospect of dressing up millions of American youth in new and more costly garments. Partly because of the institute's influence, schools across the nation were ready with The Buffalo Plan when school opened in the fall of 1957.

Dress Right was more than a way to make rebellious youth behave; in fact, the program was no doubt incapable of having any appreciable impact on juvenile delinquency. What *could* be achieved through Dress Right was a schoolwide uniformity—a homogeneity in appearance, at least, if not in attitude. And, as we have seen, the code also helped clarify the existence of social classes. In short, Dress Right was a particular response to the mixing of classes, races, and subcultures in the newly "democratized" high school.

BARRIERS

Two basic solutions were brought to bear on this problem of "mixing." The first line of defense was to minimize contact between the new arrivals and the more traditional, middle-class school populations. This was accomplished both physically and ideologically—that is, by putting people in different spaces and telling them different things.

Unlike many communities, Buffalo had largely rejected the idea of the "comprehensive" high school in favor of maintaining its elaborate system of vocational education. The reason behind this decision had been clearly stated in 1937. By not mixing "trade" and "academic" students, the "atmosphere" in each school remained "homogeneous." The sorts of "odious comparisons" that occurred in "combination" (that is, comprehensive) schools "are not noticeable here."[77] (Of course, certain students were almost entirely sheltered from such "odious comparisons" by money—money that purchased private education at Nichols School, Nardin Academy, and Buffalo Seminary.)

A different kind of barrier ensured that black youth would not threaten the white, male, working-class monopoly of the skilled trades. With a few exceptions in every institution, Buffalo's blacks were denied access to the vocational schools. Instead, they were gradually integrated into the city's academic high schools: at Fosdick-Masten Park in the 1930s, at Hutchinson-Central in the 1940s, at East High in the 1950s. Once there, they were placed on slower "tracks." Although this system seemed to be a concession to integrationist sentiment, its central purpose was to limit black access to the trades.[78]

Similarly (although beyond the theme of delinquency), certain vocational schools were designed especially for girls. Young women in Buffalo in the 1950s could train for careers in advertising, nursing, business, the clothing trades, or beauty culture. But welding, auto mechanics, plastering, and carpentry were reserved for the boys. Where both sexes went to school in the same building, separate guidance counselors—one for the girls, one for the boys—helped each

Another brick in the wall. McKinley *President*, 1954. In 1958, McKinley's assistant principal advised graduates to "avoid that first arrest."

Aspiring auto mechanics at Burgard Vocational, 1958. *Craftsman.* Burgard students were cautioned to avoid "the lofty refusal to perform some act which one might consider beneath the assumed station in life."

McKinley High School, 1948. *President.*

Buffalo Seminary, an elite, nonsectarian school for girls founded in 1851, in a photograph taken across a Frederick Law Olmsted parkway. The trees have since fallen victim to Dutch Elm disease. *The Seminaria*, 1950.

The board of the Buffalo Seminary yearbook, *The Seminaria*, beneath the image of L. Gertrude Angell, headmistress of the school from 1903 to 1952. *The Seminaria*, 1950.

group locate its proper place in the economic system.[79] In an effort to shore up a gender structure that had been collapsing since World War II, school officials also made sure that boys and girls shared as few spaces and experiences as possible. Boys and girls ate in boys' and girls' cafeterias; belonged to Senior Girls Hi-Y or Senior Boys Hi-Y; and, in at least one institution, governed the school from a Girls Small Council and a Boys Inner Council.[80]

Physical barriers were reinforced by ideology. This ideology might be present in the direct terms used by Riverside High School principal Ray Spear in addressing the class of 1955. "People are like boats," Spear commented. "Some

SEMINARIA 195

Bright Girls
Who've Won their
Fashion Honors
Select Clothes for
School, Dates and
Parties at

Berger's TEEN TOWN

In this yearbook advertisement, a downtown department store recognized youth as a distinct market and promised to turn every Seminary girl into a southern belle. *The Seminaria*, 1950.

are small and insignificant; others are large and important. Do not feel useless if you are small. The active little tugboats guide the huge ocean liners into port." Usually, however, class ideology came wrapped in the cloak of "maturity," a postwar buzzword. On its face, maturity seemed an altogether reasonable if somewhat tepid idea—a paltry ideational equivalent of a pan-American puberty celebration; and who, after all, could object to parents and educators telling the children to "grow up"?[81]

But maturity was more than that. It was an ideology differentiated by social class. As the school yearbooks of the 1950s reveal, one set of injunctions to maturity was intended for the upwardly mobile middle class, while another set was designed for the working class. At middle-class high schools such as Bishop Timon, Bennett, East, and Kensington, maturity meant social leadership, decision making, individualism, creative problem solving, an open-ended future; at working-class training centers such as Seneca, Burgard, and McKinley, maturity meant respecting authority, being presentable and personable, being satisfied with what one is and what one has.[82]

As a rite of maturity, graduation was colored by these class-linked meanings. For the middle class, graduation functioned as a beginning, an opening outward; for the working class, it was a culmination, a closing off. The prom was another

This photograph of a demonstration in a Bennett High School science class was captioned, "Ecstasy in the classroom. Every hair on her body was standing on end." *Beacon*, commencement issue, 1958. Efforts to keep boys and girls as separate as possible were perhaps a response to the high level of sexual energy present in the schools.

The girls' cafeteria at Riverside, 1952. *Skipper*. School cafeterias, like those in many factories, were usually gender segregated. In the back of the 1960 *Skipper*, amidst advertisements, was this inquiry: "Why didn't we get co-ed lunches?" Good question.

GIRLS' CAFETERIA

GUIDANCE

GIRLS
COUNSELOR

GERTRUDE
ZIEMANN

The ideology of guidance was democratic; students would make career decisions on the basis of information provided by the counselor. However, the existence of gender-typed counselors suggests how limited the freedom of decision really was. Hutchinson-Central High School, *Calendar*, 1949.

To the Boys and Girls of Hutchinson-Central:

The counseling service at Hutchinson is relatively new and up to this date has been on a part time basis. Next year it will be on a full time basis and the door of Room 256 and Room 207 will be open to you at all times.

The purpose of this service is to assist you in learning to know yourself; to help you understand your abilities and aptitudes, your interests and accomplishments, and your failings and limitations. We can provide you with accurate information concerning educational and vocational requirements and opportunities suitable to your qualifications. We will try to help you in solving your personal problems.

Your educational problems may have to do with a change in your course of study, selection of a Major, especially in the General course, a choice of electives or credits for graduation. The answers to these problems are available if you will but ask for them. If you are failing in your subjects we can give you some hints on how to improve your study habits.

Perhaps you are uncertain about the choice of a college or school after graduation from high school. There are over two hundred college catalogs available and many interesting books of views of the various colleges. In addition we have pamphlets on the offerings of technical institutes, the armed forces, and private business and trade schools. These may be seen at any time. We shall be glad to give the seniors information on scholarships which are available and to assist them in filling out applications for college entrance.

Among your vocational problems, there is perhaps no one decision so important for you to make as the decision of which path you should follow in your life work. It is your life and what you do with it in great part rests on your choice of a career. In order to make intelligent decisions in planning your life career you need to understand yourself and your opportunities. Do not hesitate to seek aid from all possible sources in making this decision.

How can you learn about yourself—your strengths and weaknesses, your likes and dislikes? Your abilities, interests and personality traits are not hidden as a rule but reveal themselves in school records, in the use of your leisure time and in daily life contacts.

Your interests, that is, your likes and dislikes, should be taken into consideration in planning your future. If you do not know what your interests are, we can give you a simple test which will help you to recognize your interest pattern, or to eliminate those fields in which you are not interested. There

8

This student apparently accepted the dominant ideology of class. Riverside *Skipper*, 1950.

"We can't all be captains, we've got to be crew,
There's something for all of us here.
There's big work to do and there's lesser to do,
And the task we must do is the near.

If you can't be a highway then just be a trail,
If you can't be the sun be a star;
It isn't by size that you win or you fail--
Be the best of whatever you are!"

--Douglas Malloch

FRESHMAN · SOPHOMORE · JUNIOR · SENIOR

Every institution presented the movement from freshman to senior as a triumphal procession to leadership, heightened responsibility, and maturity. In this cartoon, student artist Lochte captured something of this ideology while ironically suggesting the zoot-suiter as the end product. Buffalo Technical, *Techtonian*, 1947.

15 Forgetful Seniors !

Lee Brink
Gus Brooks
Howard J. Chandler
Edward Fryzowski
Richard Gruber

Arthur W. Holtz
Richard J. Hoy
Donald B. Kolacki
Gene Kubiak
Donald J. Lehr

Robert Menz
Joseph C. Setlock
Robert W. Stoness
William Wartinger
John Wawrowski

The 1956 Burgard *Craftsman* listed Robert Menz as one of fifteen seniors who had forgotten to have a senior picture taken for the yearbook. In fact, Menz had not forgotten. School principal William Kamprath had refused to allow Menz's photograph to appear, as punishment for his participation in the cherry bombing of a school toilet. Well aware of the social importance of graduation, Kamprath also warned Menz that in the event of further trouble, he "would not walk across the stage."

This generation was ready for rock 'n' roll. Riverside *Skipper*, 1948.

class-linked celebration of maturity, a sort of coming-out party sanctioned by parents and characterized by youth voluntarily shedding cultural and subcultural apparel for "adult" tuxedos and evening gowns, dancing to a traditional orchestra rather than popular records or rock 'n' roll and, in theory and outward appearance, sublimating sexuality in romance. A Timon senior perceptively described the prom not as an immediate experience of the folk culture, but as a spectacle to be remembered even as it was being lived: an "unforgettable" evening; "punch parties and breakfasts all took their place in our memory."[83]

HOMOGENEITY

To combat delinquency by erecting barriers between classes was workable but dangerous; the approach required the sort of clarification of distinctions that could easily pull apart a school, a school system, or a community. Recognizing the risks, school officials found ways to delimit fragmentation, to foster centripetal energies, and to provide students with a sense of commonality.[84]

Uniformity—or, more accurately, the appearance of uniformity—could be generated coercively, by creating an environment hostile to subcultural expressions. School officials in Buffalo forced students to wear ties or to shave beards and made every effort to keep bebop, rock 'n' roll, and other "alternative" musical styles out of the high schools. By refusing to recognize ethnic- or neighborhood-based groups or to allow them official access to school facilities, the Buffalo Board of Education sought to undercut the fraternities and sororities that continued to focus student attention beyond the school.[85]

It made more sense, however, to present this thrust toward homogeneity under the more positive and compelling frameworks of loyalty, brotherhood, democracy, and toleration. Under the doctrine of toleration, a postwar staple, racial, ethnic, and class differences were not only to be "tolerated," they were to be celebrated in assemblies, pageants, and brotherhood weeks. One school claimed to be doing its part "to 'make the world safe for differences.'"[86] These differences were to be tolerated, however, not for their own sake, not because they were good and right and important in themselves, but because toleration was the first step in achieving some larger goal, such as a conflict-free school environment, that transcended such differences. In the decade after 1945, the students at virtu-ally every high school were urged to understand their school, and the polyglot student population, as a mini United Nations, a model of the "one world" theme so popular at the time. Recognition of individual and group differences was the essential antecedent to harmonious living.

While differences were assumed to exist and to have some importance, the schools were clearly uncomfortable with the idea of applying these differences in any concrete way. At Buffalo Technical High School, for example, the Color Guard, selected by the student body, was the most prestigious school organiza-tion, held out as a model of harmonious group living under democratic pluralism. Yet the thought that students would actually select the Color Guard on the basis of group differences was anathema. In voting for the Color Guard, "no boy asks himself, as he makes his choice, 'What is his race? To which religion does he belong?' No.—the selection is made on qualities which anyone may possess." Thus students were exposed to and made aware of "differences" in order to teach the lesson that, in the end, even the most essential differences of race, class, and national origin were, in fact, of little consequence. In a world in which God had created "all men equal," the schools, at least, were "one world."[87]

Athletics served many functions in the postwar high school, not the least of which was to focus the energies of different students away from their subcultures and on the team and the institution. Interscholastic debate competitions, assem-blies, homerooms, and civics classes also generated loyalty to the institution and created the sense of a shared community and common values. The goal was the compelling brand of school spirit presented in the 1951 Seneca Vocational year-book, *The Chieftain*, which described Seneca as "a feeling, a spirit, an attitude . . . a way of life."[88]

To foster school spirit and generate loyalty to their institutions, school ad-ministrators favored forms of authority that involved students in the governance process. Between 1940 and 1960, most Buffalo schools, public and private, vocational as well as academic, created new and extensive systems of student-centered governance and discipline. The city's most elaborate system was in place at Seneca Vocational, where membership on the Tribal Council or one of several committees charged with maintaining order in the cafeteria or near the lockers seems to have been the primary extracurricular activity. At Buffalo Semi-nary, an elite private school where some form of "self-government" had been in place since 1908, the early 1950s brought student proctors for the study halls

This 1947 pageant celebrated the popular theme of "one world," while suggesting that the United States—represented by the black flag-carrying soldier—was central to that new world. The photograph also implies racial equality, ironically at a time when the American military was still segregated. Fosdick-Masten Park, *Chronicle*.

With Liberty and

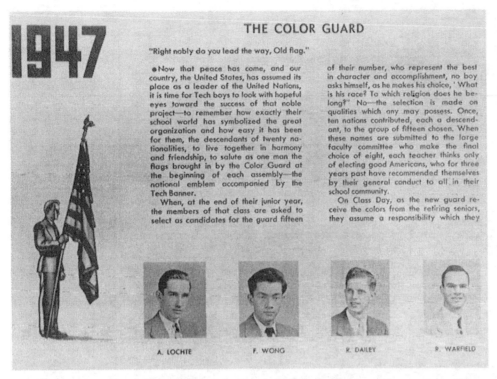

THE COLOR GUARD

"Right nobly do you lead the way, Old flag."

● Now that peace has come, and our country, the United States, has assumed its place as a leader of the United Nations, it is time for Tech boys to look with hopeful eyes toward the success of that noble project—to remember how exactly their school world has symbolized the great organization and how easy it has been for them, the descendants of twenty nationalities, to live together in harmony and friendship, to salute as one man the flags brought in by the Color Guard at the beginning of each assembly—the national emblem accompanied by the Tech Banner.

When, at the end of their junior year, the members of that class are asked to select as candidates for the guard fifteen of their number, who represent the best in character and accomplishment, no boy asks himself, as he makes his choice, ' What is his race? To which religion does he belong?' No—the selection is made on qualities which any may possess. Once, ten nations contributed, each a descendant, to the group of fifteen chosen. When these names are submitted to the large faculty committee who make the final choice of eight, each teacher thinks only of electing good Americans, who for three years past have recommended themselves by their general conduct to all in their school community.

On Class Day, as the new guard receive the colors from the retiring seniors, they assume a responsibility which they

A. LOCHTE   F. WONG   R. DAILEY   R. WARFIELD

In response to the pluralistic student populations of the 1940s, Buffalo Technical's Color Guard communicated an ideal of social harmony based on merit. *Techtonian*, 1947.

Regardless of program, the message of every assembly was that the school somehow transcended social and economic distinctions. Lafayette assemblies, such as this one in 1957, were not entirely egalitarian; by tradition, seniors occupied the best seats (a distinction the school encouraged). *Oracle.*

Members of Seneca Vocational's transportation committee confer over bus regulations, 1955. *Chieftain.* Many students participated in these governance structures because of the physical freedom they afforded.

and a new demerit system, supervised by a student judiciary board granted authority to act as "judge and jury" and to head off disciplinary problems through "informal discussion" with wayward girls. Riverside youth carried out monitoring and social service functions through a Girls Small Council (established in 1939) and a Boys Inner Council (1940). Although such organizations were labeled student "government," the government they provided was always at the discretion of school officials and generally limited to maintaining order and establishing standards of conduct and dress. In some cases, students made known their resentment at these pseudodemocratic mechanisms.[89]

In responding to what seemed a straightforward problem of juvenile delinquency—of joyriding, of stealing hubcaps, of corner lounging—public officials, church leaders, and educators found themselves at loggerheads with problems of class and race that could not be solved by moving youth off street corners,

One view of the student council at Lafayette High, 1953. Not all students accepted democratic methods at face value. *Oracle*, 1953.

censoring the media, building recreation facilities, or prohibiting levis in the classroom. What the situation called for, and what Buffalo's social engineers provided, was intervention at the level of class: on the one hand, erecting institutional and ideological barriers to protect white, middle-class youth from the working class and blacks; on the other hand, creating the illusion of the schools and the society as democratic and egalitarian. The result was a system in precarious equilibrium, held together by a tissue of ideology and contributing to the very problems it was supposed to be solving.

A home economics class at newly integrated East High, 1954. *Eastonian.* Note the racial groupings.

PORTENTS

Amid the conservatism of the late 1940s and 1950s, there were portents of the frenetic and politically charged decade that would begin, really, in 1963. An early crisis occurred at East High School in the 1953–54 academic year, when the formerly white institution was integrated with black students from Hutchinson-Central and Fosdick-Masten Park. In response, school officials created a student council, sponsored a Brotherhood Week, and, with the students who wrote the 1954 yearbook, acted as if racial tensions hardly existed. When discussing that difficult year, students and administrators alike referred to "old loyalties and rivalries," as if to suggest that the problem was less one of getting blacks and whites to live together than of school ties left behind.[90] Yet genuine integration was more difficult to achieve than school officials were willing to admit—as the clusters of black and white students in an "integrated" home economics class would indicate.

Nothing like the drug culture of the 1960s existed anywhere in the United States in the 1950s; in fact, many Buffalo youth characterize that decade as a "golden age" for youth in large part because of the absence of drugs. As one North Buffalo man recalls, "There were no drugs, there was no alcohol. . . . It was a very much happier society. I got a sweet old Irish mother. And I always tell her, 'I have no bad memories of my youth.' Yeah. She cries every time I say it." But in Buffalo as elsewhere, drugs had begun to appear in some inner-city black neighborhoods at least as early as 1950.[91]

Perhaps the most ominous signal of the end of an era would be sounded on Memorial Day 1956, less than a year after disc jockey Guy King had rung in the age of rock 'n' roll from a billboard above Shelton Square. Both events were infused with racial meaning, but from entirely different perspectives. King's act

Everyone Has a Good Time at
BEAUTIFUL, WONDERFUL

CRYSTAL BEACH

Str. Canadiana leaves Commercial St.
Daily 10 A. M., 12:15, 2:30, 5:30, 8:15,
10:30 P. M. (On Sundays no 5:30 or
10:30 boat trip.) Round Trip—Adults 99c,
Children 35c.

THE PERFECT
PICNIC PLAY-
GROUNDS
FOR GROUPS
OF ALL
KINDS!

PICNIC
GROVE
GAY MIDWAY
KIDDIELAND
FUN FOR
EVERYONE

Every Sunday, 8:15 P. M.
ROMANTIC 3-HOUR
LAKE RIDE
DANCE TO HAROLD AUSTIN'S ORCH.

announced a limited sort of integration, in which black and white musical forms
would be integrated in a package that, like Bill Haley's Comets, was indisputably
white. The second—a Memorial Day "riot" at the Crystal Beach amusement park
in Canada and on the Crystal Beach boat, the *Canadiana*—revealed a hostility
and anger among some black teenagers that belied any easy accommodation between the races and foreshadowed the more serious racial disturbances of the
1960s.

Crystal Beach Park and the *Canadiana* are fondly remembered by generations
of Buffalo youth. Memorial Day was especially significant, for it not only opened
the season at the park, but marked the beginning of Buffalo's late-arriving summer. For the city's black teenagers, Memorial Day had also become the day to
don the jackets, pants, and other items of clothing that defined membership in
a particular club or gang. Crystal Beach was one of relatively few public spaces
shared by large numbers of black and white youths (although the beach proper
was by custom reserved for whites), and the *Canadiana* voyages across Lake

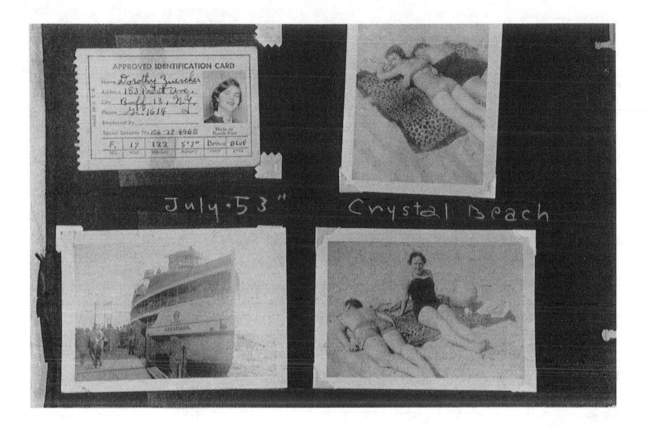

Erie were perhaps the only regular public experience in the area in which black youths were in a majority.[92]

The first sign of trouble occurred on the *Canadiana*'s 12:15 P.M. run to the amusement park, when, according to one recollection, a powerfully built black youth responded to a racial slur by striking a white soldier ("it looked like his face exploded"). "And then it started. A black guy would hit a white guy. A white guy would hit a black guy. And so on. All the way to the beach." Most accounts, however, suggest that serious conflict began several hours later, when a series of fistfights between older white and black youths in the Crystal Beach picnic area were followed by more fighting, bottle throwing, and brandishing of knives among some four-hundred teenagers massed at the park's main entrance. Canadian police eventually brought the melee under control, arresting nine youths, four of them white. Six teenagers, including two girls, were hospitalized for minor injuries.[93]

Fighting resumed on the *Canadiana*'s regular 9:15 P.M. return to Buffalo. The

Scrapbook memories of Crystal Beach and the *Canadiana*, July 1953. Courtesy, Dorothy Gallagher.

The newspaper clipping shows headlines including:

Teens Riot on Excursion Ship

Peggy Flying to Madrid To Cure Frankie's Ennui

Off-Duty Cop Held in Party Brawl Death

UN Charges Red Violations:
Order Truce Team To Quit So. Korea

Defy Cyprus Rebels, Mark 'Queen Day'

16 Hurt At Picnic

U. S. Airmen Cooling Off Hot Bus to Banbury Cross

Princess and Vivien Team-up in Hat-red

Pope, Looking Fit, Blesses Pilgrims at St Peter's Square

New York Journal-American, May 31, 1956. The "riot" received extensive coverage in the national press.

boat was carrying about a thousand people, most of them teenagers and the great majority black. Interviews conducted by the Federal Bureau of Investigation reveal that perhaps a dozen black gangs, including the Cold Spring gang, the Aces, the Frontiers, the Loews, and several girl gangs, including the Embraceables, the El Dorados, and the Queens, were aboard the boat. According to a firsthand account of the episode written for the *Courier-Express* by reporters Margaret Wynn and Dick Hirsch, "Most of the trouble was caused by gangs of Negro girls who walked the deck, attacking and molesting young white girls." The FBI interviews and oral histories confirm this interpretation, but they also reveal that much of the fighting took the form of ritualized, if potentially serious, combat between rival gangs of black males. Yet there is little doubt that something racial was happening on the *Canadiana*, and what it was is perhaps

BU 45-82

████████████████████████████
observed that these cuts ████████████████
fusely ████████████████████████
███████████████████████ He believed
that this boy, who was approximately 18 years old, was
hospitalized in Buffalo. ████████ estimated that this
incident took place at about the midway point, approximately 20 to 30 minutes before docking in Buffalo.

████████████ advised that at no time did he see
any weapons such as knives or bottles being used in any
of the fights which he observed but noted that the
Negro teen-agers were throwing numerous lighted fire-
crackers at the passengers.
███████████████████████████████
███████████████████████████████

████████ was of the opinion that all the
trouble was caused by the Negro teen-age girls who
instigated most of the fights with Negro teen-age males
or the white persons involved in any fight. ████████
said that the Negro youths would fall behind the Negro
girls and would join in any fracas that the Negro girls
got into.

████████████ said that he could not possibly say
whether the following girl groups were the leaders in
any of the incidents which took place but added that they
were conspicuous aboard the ship. These groups which
consist of Negro teen-age girls were identified as follows:

> "The Embraceables" - wear jackets that
> are deep purple with pink lettering;
> at least 6 of these observed.

> "The El Dorados" - wear dark jackets with
> green lettering. ████████ also observed
> some Negro teen-age boys wearing these
> jackets.

> "The Queens" - wear jackets, color not
> recalled by ████████ with replicas of
> 4 playing cards, the queens of every
> suit on the back of these jackets.

17

Testimony gathered by the FBI during its inquiry into the *Canadiana* incident. When victims and witnesses proved unable (or unwilling) to identify assailants, officials declined prosecution. This and other documents were obtained through a Freedom of Information Act request.

best captured in the recollection of a white man from North Buffalo who was approached by black youths asking the question, What color am I? "If you'd say, 'Well, you look brown,' they'd say, 'I'm black. I'm not a Negro or a coon, I'm black.' It was the first time I'd heard the word 'black.' "[94]

About forty fearful white youth, including several who had been beaten or cut, chose to weather the voyage in the ship's dining room. One, asked why he had come below, replied, "Only a crazy man would stay up there, and I ain't crazy. And besides," he added, "that isn't a fight, it's a race riot." And that, of course, was the question. Was it a "race riot" or wasn't it? Witnesses and participants inevitably acknowledged that blacks and whites fought each other at the park and on the boat, yet there was some doubt about whether this confirmed the existence of a race riot. A black man, arrested for participating in the Crystal Beach skirmish, recalls experiencing racial prejudice in Buffalo only after 1960, following a tour of duty with the Marines. For him, the word "riot" was an inappropriate label applied by Buffalo police to conflict that was in essence territorial: "You fought for the neighborhood you came from."[95]

Despite Wynn and Hirsch's powerful account, Buffalo's public officials and community leaders invariably discounted the racial content of the incident, locating the cause of the event in youth rather than race and calling on some version of the now-familiar ideology of toleration to downplay the issue of racial antagonism. A subcommittee of the Board of Community Relations emphasized that the fighting had sprung from the decision of two black gangs to settle their differences at Crystal Beach, and that when this confrontation had failed to materialize, "the stage was set for almost anything." Speaking for the city's black community, the *Buffalo Criterion* found the Memorial Day episode "a regretful occurrence for the City of Good Neighbors" and reasoned that because the affair was unplanned it "cannot be considered, as such, a race riot." The city's white leaders, just as eager to devalue evidence of a racial problem, generally understood the Memorial Day violence as a particularly virulent episode in the history of youth culture: a case of "flagrant hoodlumism" caused by "undisciplined" and irresponsible "young punks" bent on defying authority. In an editorial that denied even the *possibility* that youth could make a significant social statement, the *Buffalo Evening News* labeled the *Canadiana* incident "strictly a juvenile performance," in which the "conspicuous absence of any adult participation or incitement clearly refutes any too-easy assumption that the underlying problem was a breakdown in community race relations."[96]

Nonetheless, the community could not be swayed from seeing the Memorial Day violence in racial terms. The *Canadiana*, its reputation irrevocably damaged, finished the season but was not carrying passengers to Crystal Beach the following Memorial Day. At the Zanzibar Lounge, the large, racially mixed crowds of past years thinned as a result of the *Canadiana* riot. "We had Illinois Jacquet," recalls the Zanzibar's owner, "and we couldn't draw flies." In 1960, the club closed. Where black and white youth continued to come in contact—at rock concerts, Golden Gloves matches, at movie theaters, and on the city streets —racial violence became increasingly common, culminating in December 1957 in a stabbing of white ushers at the downtown Center Theater during the showing of the rock 'n' roll film, *Jamboree*.[97] And in 1961, when Hi-Teen folded after fifteen years of Saturday "club" meetings, the city lost still another public space (albeit largely white), and with it some sense of itself as a whole community with shared values.

What is tragic about this is that there was some genuine potential for social progress in the contacts that were taking place among Buffalo youths. In the early 1950s, blacks and whites were willing to share space, whether on the deck of the *Canadiana*, at the roller-skating rink, at the Zanzibar, in Memorial Auditorium, or in the neighborhoods. To realize this potential, Buffalo's leadership had to stop running from the obvious problems these same contacts created and to press forward toward a community that was genuinely integrated. This proved too much to expect, and when the sun went down on Memorial Day in 1956, the potential was gone.[98]

In interpreting the *Canadiana* riot as an episode involving age rather than race or class, Buffalo's public officials and leaders were once again denying—at least for public consumption—the central social realities of the age. In calling upon the construct "City of Good Neighbors," the city's leaders were following in the footsteps of school officials who had earlier summoned students to understand their schools as meccas of pluralistic toleration.

If, indeed, it is appropriate to understand the *Canadiana* incident as primarily a racial incident—and if, instead, authorities preferred to see it as the product of hoodlumism—then we might ask if the postwar effort to understand youth crime as "juvenile delinquency" was not also misguided. This is not to say that school buildings were not vandalized and cars not stolen; these acts occurred, and in numbers sufficient to warrant concern. What is at issue is whether they were committed by youths acting as youth, or by black youths acting as blacks, by

to revenue
was $5000
In another
nd Joseph
Lewiston
ica for "$1

ment, two
of the Bu-
vestigation,
ctive Unit,
n Lockport
gging into
Magaddino

d Jury

ters is in
lachin, and
ara County
were "gath-
vill be pre-
grand jury
in Tioga
y into the

, continued
.)

OSES
YEARS

ening News
Ont., Dec.
to pass
this year
downbound
arliest clos-
p Canal in

oc will tie
t midweek
e's winter
tching last

Named

16 (AP) —
f Syracuse
nan of the
l. He was
the final
s 20th an-
ce.

Wounded Ushers Tell of Brawl During Rock 'n' Roll Movie

Four Are Stabbed, Fifth Injured in Battle In Center Theater; Crude Weapons Found

Hoodlums stabbed four youths and injured a fifth when a matinee in Center Theater erupted into a near riot shortly after 4 o'clock Sunday afternoon.

Two suspects were held and police recovered a small arsenal of crude weapons. The melee was the worst of several that have

Pictures on the Picture Page.

broken out during downtown showings of rock 'n' roll films during the past year.

Injured were:

Paul F. Rush Jr., 17, of 155 Waltercrest, Terr., West Seneca, an usher, admitted to Columbus Hospital with knife wounds of the left shoulder and left upper back.

Robert Rush, 16, his brother, also an usher, admitted to the same hospital with a stab wound of the lower back.

Daniel Majchrzak, 15, of 1325 Walden Ave., Cheektowaga, another usher, treated in Emergency Hospital for nose and head injuries.

Barry Cave, 18, of 2987 Seneca St., West Seneca, an usher, treated in Emergency Hospital for a knife wound of the lower back and a probable fractured nose. He was released, but was to return today for further examination.

Edward C. Cranford, 15, of 415 Hickory St., a patron, treated in Columbus Hospital for a knife wound of the left arm. Police said he was an innocent bystander who was trying to get clear of the trouble area. He was released after treatment in the hospital.

Held without charge were youths booked as:

John Settle, 16, of 490 Woodlawn Ave.

Donald L. Prillerman, 16, of 42 Butler Ave.

"Helpless and Surrounded"

"We were helpless and surrounded," Paul Rush said, describing the brawl to a News reporter. "They seemed to come from all over and I don't know how we got out. I never even knew I was cut until the fight ended."

(Two Held, continued on Page 22, Column 3.)

ATLAS LAUNCHING DELAYED, POSSIBLY UNTIL TOMORROW

CAPE CANAVERAL, Fla., Dec. 16 (AP)—An attempt to launch the Atlas intercontinental ballistic missile today has been postponed, possibly until tomorrow.

Scattering groups of watchers on the beach near this closely guarded missile center dispersed as the postponement of firing became evident.

The Atlas was undergoing its final pre-flight "count down" when the postponement came shortly after noon.

Two of the giant missiles were visible in their stands. These may be the ones which were given static tests last week.

Two previous test launchings of the Atlas were held last summer and last fall.

In both instances the missile got into the air. Before it could get fully under way, however, it started to wobble and change ccurse and had to be blown apart.

The Atlas is designed to deliver a hydrogen warhead over an arc reaching as high as 600 miles above the earth to a target 5000 miles or more from its launching point. Its average speed is 10,000 miles an hour.

...mpel Registration ...als Ruled Invalid

...rt, in 5-4 Decision, Declares ...City Ordinance Unconstitutional

Press
. 16—The
ay struck
Angeles or-
rsons con-
gister with

d 47 mu-

The Los Angeles ordinance, adopted in 1933, was attacked by Virginia Lambert, who in 1951 was convicted of forgery and put on probation. In 1952 the probation order was changed to require her to spend six months in jail.

On Feb. 2, 1955, she was ac-

Frontier Has Had 14 Bank Holdups In Past Three Years

Biggest Loot Was $52,590 on Feb. 15, 1956, at Clinton-Bailey; Last Was in September

Today's robbery was the 14th bank holdup on the Niagara Frontier in less than three years. Six of the holdups have been in offices of the Manufacturers & Traders Trust Co.

Biggest loot in the last three years was $52,590 taken from the M&T's Clinton-Bailey office Feb. 15, 1956.

Other M&T holdups in the last three years were:

May 18, 1955 — Portage Rd. branch, Niagara Falls, $5700.

June 14, 1955—Main office, Main and Swan, $2059.

Aug. 8, 1955—Thruway Plaza branch, $11,000.

July 9, 1956—Adam, Meldrum & Anderson store branch, $2047.

Sept. 18, 1957 — Main-Tupper branch, $6838.

Other bank holdups in the last three years were:

Jan. 25, 1955—Power City Trust office, Marine Trust Co., Niagara Falls, $995.

April 22, 1955—Jefferson Savings & Loan Association, 1369 Jefferson, $2879.

June 8, 1955—Buffalo Savings Bank, Main and Genesee, $2289.

July 18, 1955—Buffalo Savings Bank, Main and Genesee, $2179.

May 29, 1956—First Federal Savings & Loan Association, 2133 Genesee, $1024.

July 18, 1956—New York Central Federal Credit Union office, New York Central Station, $668.

Oct. 2, 1956—Linwood Branch, Liberty Bank, $23,775.10.

California Capitol's Roof Leaks

SACRAMENTO, Calif., Dec. 16 (AP)—A bucket brigade worked in the State Capitol Sunday after rain water poured through leaks in the roof, flooded several offices and dripped into the Senate chamber. Workers used waste baskets to catch the water.

Avalanches Isolate 3 Villages

revolver to
told him:
"Keep yo
you won't g
Mr. Rupp
passageway
tellers' win
the gunman
"Don't a
the manage
held up."
At that
companion
entrance an
paper shopp
The gunm
the line of
cash drawer
tellers' posi
the teller
alow him t
The teller
Highland
Ont.; Miss C
448 Herkim
laide French

Six Patrons

After wal
behind the
walked bac
position —
the drawer
opened. Pul
discovered
which he s
"You're a
Mr. Hinton.
However,
the teller f
His comp
doorway, k
his pockets.
play a gun.
About six
were frozen
ing the robl
About a
robbery, po
car at Orton
in the belie
the getaway
The men
the bank are
of 1956 or l
lice receive
the escape

May Have R

Witnesses
number beg
would indic
car.
The holdu
as white an
gloves.
One was
tall with b
eyes. He
blue sweate
The other
5 feet 5 in
hair, khaki
His weight
pounds.
The two

Buffalo Evening News, December 16, 1957. Like the *Canadiana* incident, the violence at the Center Theater was caused by more than youthful excess. The film *Jamboree* appealed to both whites and blacks; at issue, from the perspective of black teenagers, was the right of whites to appropriate black music for their own purposes. Used with the permission of Murray B. Light, editor and senior vice-president, *The Buffalo News*.

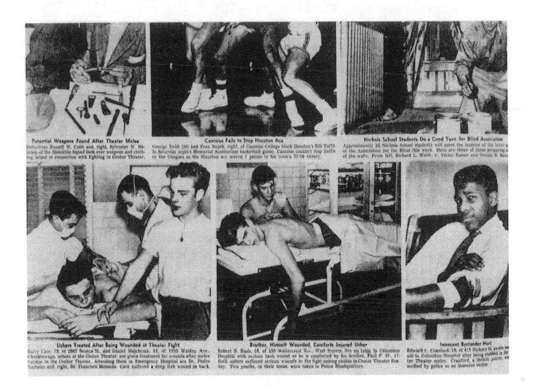

Potential Weapons Found After Theater Melee
Detectives Russell W. Cobb and, right, Sylvester W. De-laney of the Homicide Squad look over weapons and cloth-ing seized in connection with fighting in Center Theater.

Canisius Fails to Stop Houston Ace
George Swift (20) and Fran Rejek, right, of Canisius College block Houston's Bill Tuffli in Saturday night's Memorial Auditorium basketball game. Canisius couldn't stop Tuffli as the Cougars as the Houston ace scored 7 points in his team's 77-70 victory.

Nichols School Students Do a Good Turn for Blind Association
Approximately 25 Nichols School students will paint the interior of the house of the Association for the Blind this week. Here are three of them preparing one of the walls. From left, Richard L. Webb, C. Victor Raiser and Dennis R. Mann.

Ushers Treated After Being Wounded in Theater Fight
Barry Case, 19, of 2907 Seneca St., and Daniel Majkrzak, 18, of 1355 Walden Ave., Cheektowaga, ushers at the Center Theater, are given treatment for wounds after melee Sunday in the Center Theater. Attending them in Emergency Hospital are Dr. Pedro Sarlatea and, right, Dr. Franciszo Menachi. Case suffered a deep stab wound in back.

Brother, Himself Wounded, Comforts Injured Usher
Robert R. Bush, 16, of 159 Wildersweet Ter., West Seneca, lies on table in Columbus Hospital with serious back wound as he is comforted by his brother, Paul P. Jr., 17. Both ushers suffered serious wounds in the fight among youths in Center Theater Sunday. Two youths, in their teens, were taken to Police Headquarters.

Innocent Bystander Hurt
Edward C. Crawford, 19, of 415 Hickory St., awaits aid in Columbus Hospital after being stabbed in the Center Theater melee. Crawford, a theater patron, was described by police as an innocent victim.

working-class youths acting as the working class, and by middle-class youths acting out of motivations that had to do with membership in the middle class in the 1950s.

Here is where history can help. Taken in isolation, the incidents at Crystal Beach and on the *Canadiana* could reasonably be understood as the idiosyn-cratic product of the delinquent side of an irresponsible youth culture. Many participants interpreted the events in just those terms. However, placed in the context of the civil rights revolution of the 1960s, the same events become an early warning of the racial troubles that would rock Buffalo and other cities a decade later. The angry black youths roaming the decks of the *Canadiana* would be seen again at Watts; their opponents would reappear in the antibusing mobs of the 1970s, the hard-hat component of the white backlash.

The term "juvenile delinquency" is flawed, then, because it implies motivation and subsumes analysis; it implies that all acts committed under the rubric of juvenile delinquency were committed by aimless youth acting fundamentally out of some age-related impulse. The term "youth culture" is not much better. In fact, it might be best defined as an educated version of "juvenile delinquency," since it, too, implies that whatever culture might be observed among teenagers is immediately to be understood as a function of "youth." To the extent that youth-culture analysis acknowledges that teenagers might have political ideas, their politics are easily dismissed as the immature gestures of the not-fully-grown.

In just the same way, the concept of youth culture tempts us to treat in some unified fashion things that might otherwise seem quite different: Elvis Presley and Perry Como; pegged pants and poodle skirts; the Gunners and Tau Zeta Tau; Hi-Teen and "Hound Dog" Lorenz; the white and black youths who locked horns on the *Canadiana*. To the uninitiated and the fearful, to the anxious parent and the beleaguered policeman of the 1950s, such connections seemed reasonable enough. On any other basis, they appear forced and simplistic.

Let us briefly reexamine the incidents that open and close this essay: Guy King's manic celebration of "Rock Around the Clock," and the trouble on the *Canadiana*. A "youth culture" approach to these events might note that one event was peaceful and the other violent, but that both were products of teen-age thoughtlessness and disrespect for authority. A "subculture" approach would also seek to give the events some logical relation, but of a different sort. Under this framework, the *Canadiana* incident becomes in some measure a confrontation between white working-class and black subcultures, acting on ideas first expressed in neighborhood struggles that were in turn the product of urban popu-lation migrations. Thus the *Canadiana* riot can be seen as a logical extension of earlier racial incidents in the Masten-Southampton neighborhood.

King's stunt seems at first to deny the notion of subculture, because its focus, Bill Haley's recording of "Rock Around the Clock," has since come to stand not just for all American youth at one moment in the mid-1950s, but for the very concept of that decade as a golden age of cultural homogeneity (the "Happy Days" idea). Yet the song achieved great popularity only when it appeared in the film *Blackboard Jungle*, where it stood *not* for a generalized opposition to authority but for a proletariat of black, white, and brown teenagers trapped in North Manual Trades High School.[99] At the risk of introducing contradictions, we should also reflect on the country-based *whiteness* of Haley's brand of rock 'n' roll and, following through on this line of argument, on Haley as a symbol of rock 'n' roll as a form of cultural imperialism, filtering and sifting black music and lyrics to make them palatable to a white audience. Either way (and this hardly exhausts the possibilities) Guy King's billboard broadcast becomes an expression of subculture, not youth culture. As subcultural expressions, the two events can also be understood not as chronological bookends, representing a glorious beginning and a tragic ending (indeed, the events are too close in time to make such a proposition compelling), but as signs in a complex and flawed cultural matrix, always on the verge of self-destruction, held together with the bailing wire of social engineering.

The authorities of the 1950s—city officials, police, educators, the churches, parents—could hardly have been expected to appreciate "Rock Around the Clock" as a white advance over the contested terrain of popular music, or to understand pink and black drapes as an expression of working-class opposition to middle-class notions of style and fashion. It made more sense, and was less threatening, to attribute offending behavior either to "youth" or "juvenile delinquency" and, having thereby dispensed with its serious content, to try to get rid of it. Get the kids off the street corners. Pass a school dress code. Take rock 'n' roll off the air. Deny fraternities and sororities access to school facilities.

Still, there is evidence that these same authorities were not entirely lacking in understanding of the core elements of class and race. The Buffalo Youth Board's statistics clearly located delinquency by patterns of income and class. Reporters Wynn and Hirsch presented the *Canadiana* riot in unmistakably racial terms. The ideology of maturity was nothing less than a discussion of the responsibilities and opportunities of class. The system of vocational and academic schools, and the Dress Right code that provided for different standards for each type of institution, are evidence of a citywide investment in social class.

In their search for a society that would retain its historical social character and yet seem democratic and comfortably homogeneous, Buffalo's social engineers sometimes papered over the class, racial, and ethnic divisions that were at the core of the city's "youth" problem. The stellar example, of course, is the response of city leaders to the *Canadiana* riot, but the schools were the most crucial arena. Traumatic conflicts of race were met with pleas for school unity and subsumed in a doctrine of toleration that acknowledged differences only to render them innocuous. Calls for a new maturity encouraged youth of all social classes to see themselves and their problems as part of a transcendent process of growing up. Fraternities and sororities that seemed to interfere with the school's homogenizing mission were officially discouraged. In the end, the grievances and frustrations that were part of coming of age in postwar Buffalo were repressed and shoved aside, to emerge a decade later in a new and more virulent form that could not so easily be written off as one more expression of the culture of youth.

NOTES

1. "Broadcast Beat," *Buffalo Evening News* (no date), in WGR clipping collection, WGR, Buffalo, New York; "Disc Jockey Atop Sign Causes Jam in Shelton Square," *Buffalo Evening News*, July 5, 1955, p. 6; "Teen-Agers Jam Main St. to See Antics Broadcast," *Buffalo Evening News*, May 9, 1955, sec. 2, p. 21.

2. The subcultural approach used in this book is derived from the work of the Centre for Contemporary Cultural Studies at the University of Birmingham, known as the "Birmingham School." The most important collection is Stuart Hall and Tony Jefferson, eds., *Resistance Through Rituals: Youth Subcultures in Postwar Britain* (London: Hutchinson, 1975). See also Mike Brake, *The Sociology of Youth Culture and Youth Subcultures: Sex and Drugs and Rock 'n' Roll?* (London: Routledge & Kegan Paul, 1980). The best critique of the concept of youth culture is John Clarke, Stuart Hall, Tony Jefferson, and Brian Roberts, "Subcultures, Cultures and Class," in Hall and Jefferson, *Resistance Through Rituals*, pp. 15–27.

3. Edward M. Bruner, "Experience and Its Expressions," in *The Anthropology of Experience*, ed. Victor W. Turner and Edward M. Bruner (Urbana: University of Illinois Press, 1986), p. 12.

4. Raymond Williams, *Problems in Materialism and Culture* (London: Verso, 1980), p. 38.

5. Stuart Hall, Dorothy Hobson, Andrew Lowe, and Paul Willis, eds., *Culture, Media, Language* (London: Hutchinson, 1980), p. 27; Brake, *Sociology of Youth Culture*, p. 68.

6. John Clarke, "Style," in Hall and Jefferson, *Resistance Through Rituals*, pp. 177–78; Brake, *Sociology of Youth Culture*, p. 158; Dick Hebdige, *Subculture: The Meaning of Style* (London: Methuen, 1979), pp. 103–4; Erica Carter, "Alice in the Consumer Wonderland: West German Case Studies in Gender and Consumer Culture," in *Gender and Generation*, ed. Angela McRobbie and Mica Nava (London: Macmillan, 1984), p. 212; Janice Radway, *Reading the Romance: Women, Patriarchy, and Popular Literature* (Chapel Hill: University of North Carolina Press, 1984), pp. 17–18, 212, 222.

7. Joseph F. Kett, *Rites of Passage: Adolescence in America, 1790 to the Present* (New York: Basic Books, 1977); Robert M. Mennel, *Thorns & Thistles: Juvenile De-*

linquents in the United States, 1825–1940
(Hanover, N.H.: The University Press of
New England, 1973); Christine Stansell,
City of Women: Sex and Class in New York,
1789–1860 (New York: Knopf, 1986), esp.
chapter 10, "The Uses of the Streets"; *Teen-*
Age Culture, ed. Jessie Bernard, *The Annals*
of the American Academy of Political and
Social Science, vol. 338 (Philadelphia,
1961); U.S. Interior Department, Office of
Education, "High School Fraternities," *Re-*
port of the Commissioner of Education for
the Year Ended June 30, 1907 (Washington,
D.C., 1908), vol. 1, pp. 438–41; Mad-
line Kinter Remmlein, "Can High School
Fraternities Exist Legally," *Bulletin of the*
National Association of Secondary School
Principals 31 (Feb. 1947): 51–69; David
Tyack, Robert Lowe, and Elisabeth Hansot,
Public Schools in Hard Times: The Great
Depression and Recent Years (Cambridge,
Mass.: Harvard University Press, 1984),
pp. 144–45; Paula S. Fass, *The Damned*
and the Beautiful: American Youth in the
1920's (New York: Oxford University Press,
1977); Kenneth E. Reid, *From Character*
Building to Social Treatment: The History of
the Use of Groups in Social Work (Westport,
Conn.: Greenwood Press, 1981), appendix
2; Jane Addams, "The Spirit of Youth and
the City Streets," in *The Social Thought of*
Jane Addams, ed. Christopher Lasch (New
York: Bobbs-Merrill, 1965), p. 90.

8. James Gilbert, *A Cycle of Outrage:*
America's Reaction to the Juvenile Delin-
quent in the 1950s (New York: Oxford
University Press, 1986), p. 21.

9. David Nasaw, *Schooled to Order: A*
Social History of Public Schooling in the
United States (New York: Oxford Univer-

sity Press, 1979), p. 163; Gilbert, *Cycle of*
Outrage, pp. 18–19.

10. Buffalo and Erie County, Council of
Social Agencies, Leisure Time Interests
Committee, "Survey of Recreational Needs
and Facilities in Buffalo and Erie County,"
mimeographed, 1946–1949, pp. 2, 3.

11. Clippings in Butler-Mitchell Boys
Club Scrapbook, 1942–47, Butler-Mitchell
Boys Club, Buffalo; Shirley Peterson,
"Nation's Youth Facing Future of Uncer-
tainty," *Buffalo Courier-Express*, Oct. 20,
1946; Leroy E. Fess, "Boys at Camp to Help
Harvest Area's Crops," no paper identi-
fied; and "Action Taken to Ease Farm Labor
Crisis," Aug. 29, 1943, no paper. Robert T.
Bapst, address to Public School No. 6
graduating class, 1943, copy in School 31
Collection, Buffalo, 3d floor.

12. *Buffalo Criterion*, "Youth's Decision,
and the Future" (editorial), Sept. 30, 1944,
p. 2; editorial, Aug. 19, 1944.

13. Rupert Wilkinson, *American Tough:*
The Tough-Guy Tradition and American
Character (Westport, Conn.: Greenwood
Press, 1984), p. 107; Donald J. Mrozek,
"The Cult and Ritual of Toughness in Cold
War America," in *Rituals and Ceremonies*
in Popular Culture, ed. Roy B. Browne
(Bowling Green, Ohio: Bowling Green Uni-
versity Popular Press, 1980), pp. 187–88.
See also Gerald Early, "The Romance of
Toughness: La Motta and Graziano," *The*
Antioch Review 45 (Fall 1987): 385–408.

14. Peterson, "Nation's Youth Facing
Future of Uncertainty."

15. Riverside High School survey, *The*
Skipper, 1945; Gail Whitman, interview by
William Graebner, Dec. 9, 1985. (Unless
otherwise noted, all other interviews in-

cluded here were conducted by Graebner.)

16. The following paragraphs are adapted from William Graebner, "The Cold War: A Yearbook Perspective," Organization of American Historians *Magazine of History* 2 (Summer 1986): 10–14.

17. Robert Wiebe, *The Segmented Society: An Introduction to the Meaning of America* (New York: Oxford University Press, 1975), p. 201.

18. Graebner, "The Cold War."

19. Ibid.

20. For example, McKinley High School, *The President*, 1943, p. 43.

21. Graebner, "The Cold War." Of course, not all teenagers were idealistic and not all could spout the virtues of democracy or wax eloquent on the benefits of individualism at the drop of a yearbook editor's hat. In fact, postwar youth culture might be interpreted as a movement opposed in its basic substance to the ideological and political requirements of mainstream postwar America. In its concern with lifestyle, youth culture could be interpreted as a retreat into the self, into style over substance, and therefore as a rejection of, and withdrawal from, politics and ideology. By seeming to withdraw from political discourse, both abstract artists and culture-oriented teenagers appeared to strike out at a central tenet of democracy and became the object of the concern and censure of public authorities.

22. Carl Belz, *The Story of Rock*, 2nd ed. (New York: Harper Colophon Books, 1972), pp. 53–56. See also Evan Hunter, *The Blackboard Jungle* (1953; reprint, New York: Avon Books, 1976), pp. 175–83.

23. The material on Hi-Teen is adapted from William Graebner, "The 'Containment' of Juvenile Delinquency: Social Engineering and American Youth Culture in the Postwar Era," *American Studies* 27, no. 1 (Spring 1986): 81–97. © 1986 Mid-America American Studies Association. Used by permission.

24. *Courier-Express*, May 5, 1953, p. 20; *Buffalo Evening News*, March 13, 1953, p. 32; Burton Glaser interview, 1983; "The Hound-Dogs Howl" newsletter, Apr. 1956.

25. Lee Johansson interview, Aug. 22, 1985.

26. David Holdsworth interview, Aug. 22, 1984; Johansson interview; Bob Menz interview, June 28, 1983; Dave Schnell interview, Aug. 22, 1984.

27. J. Don Schlaerth, radio-TV column, *Courier-Express*, Sept. 5, 1957, in WGR clipping book, WGR, Buffalo; Margaret Wynn, *Courier-Express*, Apr. 2, 1957, pp. 1–2; Sturgis Hendrick, "Radio and TV News," *Buffalo Evening News*, Jan. 10, 1958, p. 24; *Buffalo Evening News*, Jan. 18, 1958, sec. 2, p. 3.

28. *Buffalo Evening News*, Dec. 18, 1957, p. 73; Van Miller interview, July 13, 1983; Kay Lapping interview, July 13, 1983.

29. Clipping, J. Don Schlaerth, "WEBR Record Hops Are 'the Most' for Teen-Agers," *Courier-Express*, February 23, 1958, in Danny McBride Scrapbook; flier for clients advertising on record hop broadcasts, May 21, 1958, McBride Scrapbook; Danny McBride interview, July 5, 1983.

30. Letter, Joe Allen, Jr. to Danny McBride, March 18, 1958, in McBride Scrapbook; McBride interview.

31. Seneca Vocational High School,

Chieftain, 1952, p. 75; East High School, *Eastonian*, 1951, p. 41, and 1956, p. 82. See also *Eastonian*, 1952, p. 64. Burgard High School *Craftsman*, 1954, "Class History"; 1955, "Class History"; and 1956, photographs of marching band, dance band, and accordion band; William Davenport, East High *Eastonian*, 1958, p. 6.

32. Clarke, Hall, Jefferson, and Roberts, "Subcultures, Cultures and Class," p. 12; Brake, *Sociology of Youth Culture*, p. 7.

33. Williams, *Problems in Materialism*, pp. 41, 43.

34. For zoot suit riots, Richard Polenberg, *War and Society: The United States, 1941–1945* (New York: Lippincott, 1972), p. 130. See also George Lipsitz, *Class and Culture in Cold War America: "A Rainbow at Midnight"* (South Hadley, Mass.: J. F. Bergin, 1982), pp. 25–28; and Mauricio Mazón, *The Zoot-Suit Riots: The Psychology of Symbolic Annihilation* (Austin: University of Texas Press, 1984). On hegemony, see Hebdige, *Subculture*.

35. Johansson interview, July 20, 1983; Ray Spasiano interview, July 20, 1983; Dan Petrelli interview, Nov. 29, 1985; Holdsworth interview; Al Triem interview, Aug. 2, 1984; Jerry Szefel interview, Aug. 15, 1984. A 1962 study claimed that color in clothes was of more importance to Negro than to white girls; cited in Mary Shaw Ryan, *Clothing: A Study in Human Behavior* (New York: Holt, Rinehart and Winston, 1966), p. 280.

36. Ralph T. Powers interview, July 12, 1983; Holdsworth interview. According to Alison Lurie, "All obviously geometrical patterns, including stripes, checks and regularly spaced images of anything from aardvarks to zinnias, seem to be related to the wish to order the universe in some way.

Stripes, for example, often seem to express organized effort, a desire or ability to 'follow the line' laid out by oneself or others" (*The Language of Clothes* [New York: Random House, 1981], p. 206).

37. Seneca Vocational High School, *The Chieftain*, 1956, p. 19. A 1953 senior, noted for his blue suede shoes, was appropriately nicknamed "Bop"; Seneca *Chieftain*, 1953, p. 12. On the influence of lower-class culture on middle-class style, see William Kvaraceus and Walter B. Miller, "Norm-Violating Behavior in Middle-Class Culture," in *Middle-Class Juvenile Delinquency*, ed. Edmund W. Vaz (New York: Harper & Row, 1967), pp. 236–40.

38. Dorothy Gallagher interview, Feb. 5, 1986; Wilson Carey McWilliams, *The Idea of Fraternity in America* (Berkeley and Los Angeles: University of California Press, 1973), p. 19; Carol Sue Roll interview, Dec. 7, 1985 (quotation); Bennett High School *Beacon*, 1957 (commencement issue), no page; Whitman interview (quotation).

39. Triem interview; Walter Marquart interview, Oct. 30, 1985; Al Marquart interview, Nov. 11, 1985; Al Marquart interview; Triem interview; patterns and patches in possession of Broadway Knitting Mills.

40. Gallagher interview; *Courier-Express*, Apr. 26, 1961, p. 1; May 30, 1951, p. 31; Dec. 29, 1951, pp. 1, 5; Aug. 26, 1954, pp. 1, 2; Apr. 20, 1955, p. 1; Federal Bureau of Investigation, File no. 45-9285, p. 17; *Buffalo Evening News*, Aug. 11, 1960, p. 27.

41. Patricia Guarino interview, Aug. 15, 1984; Martin interview.

42. Bob Prince interview, Aug. 15, 1984; "Two Hurt as Teenage Gangs Battle with

Rocks, Sticks / 16 Youths Held," *Courier-Express*, Sept. 2, 1953, p. 1; Johansson interview; Roll interview; Spain drawing in possession of William Graebner; *Courier-Express*, Sept. 3, 1953, pp. 1–2; Martin interview; "Two Hurt . . ."

43. Petrelli interview; Triem interview (quotation).

44. Angela McRobbie and Jenny Garber, "Girls and Subcultures," in Hall and Jefferson, *Resistance Through Rituals*, p. 211; June Bihl interview, Aug. 10, 1984; Johnnie Mayo photograph; Johnnie Mayo interview, Aug. 15, 1986; Prince interview; Martin interview; Erik H. Erikson, "Youth: Fidelity and Diversity," in his *The Challenge of Youth* (1963; Garden City, N.Y.: Anchor Books, 1965), p. 20.

45. Robert F. Depczynski interview, June 2, 1985; Danny Chudoba interview, June 4, 1985.

46. Raymond Williams, *Culture* (Glasgow: Fontana, 1981), pp. 205, 29.

47. My thanks to George Browder for information on Mussolini's Black Shirts. See also Paul A. Carter, *Another Part of the Fifties* (New York: Columbia University Press), pp. 99, 23; and Lurie, *Language of Clothes*, pp. 188, 192. On the police action: "Teen-agers Tell of Big Gang Fight Scheduled Tonight," *Buffalo Evening News*, Aug. 30, 1955, p. 1; "Police Fearing Fight Oust Dozen from Street Dance," *Courier-Express*, Aug. 31, 1955, pp. 1–2 (Tutuska quotation); Depczynski interview; "Black-Shirted Youths Barred from Dance in Move to Stop Fight," *Buffalo Evening News*, Aug. 31, 1955, p. 43. On the T-shirt ban: Chudoba interview; Triem interview; B. John Tutuska interview, May 29, 1985. See also Depczynski interview; Johansson interview; Bob Sniatecki interview, Aug. 15, 1984; and Frank Sedita, Jr., interview, Sept. 9, 1985. Several sources claim the T-shirt ban was announced in the newspapers; I have been unable to locate any such announcement.

48. The material on fraternities and sororities is adapted from William Graebner, "Outlawing Teenage Populism: The Campaign Against Secret Societies in the American High School, 1900–1960," *Journal of American History* 74 (September 1987): 411–35.

49. Victor W. Turner, *The Ritual Process: Structure and Anti-Structure* (Chicago: Aldine, 1969), pp. 94 (quotation), 95–97, 103, 168, 171; Gail Whitman's photo, marked, "Larry, Me, Ron," in author's possession, shows the penny-laden tape.

50. Virginia Kelley collection (photographs in author's possession).

51. Herbert Marcuse, *One-Dimensional Man: Studies in the Ideology of Advanced Industrial Society* (Boston: Beacon Press, 1964), p. 11. On secrecy and its role in youth culture, see Paul Goodman, *Compulsory Mis-education and the Community of Scholars* (New York: Knopf, 1964), p. 72. Guarino interview (quotation).

52. Stanley Aronowitz, *False Promises: The Shaping of American Working Class Consciousness* (New York: McGraw-Hill, 1973), p. 83; Triem interview.

53. On the slumber party, see Aronowitz, *False Promises*, p. 83; on bedroom culture, see Iain Chambers, *Urban Rhythms: Pop Music and Popular Culture* (New York: St. Martin's Press, 1985), pp. 41–44; on interiority, see Mica Nava, "Youth Service Provision, Social Order and the Question of Girls," in *Gender and Generation*, ed.

McRobbie and Nava, p. 11. Boys' subculture and girls' subculture were no doubt profoundly shaped by a system of vocational education that functioned to segregate the sexes. Burgard Vocational Principal William Kamprath suggested how vocational education might forge male bonds of intimacy when he referred to Burgard's World War II training program as a "stag party." There is, Kamprath said in 1957, "no better education for a boy than a friendship of his own choosing with a schoolmaster whom he respects and likes" (Sue Fruchtbaum, "Bill Kamprath Took Printing Press, Wrecked Plane and Built a School," *Buffalo Evening News*, Nov. 16, 1957, TV section, p. 1). See also Barbara Brenzel, Cathy Roberts-Gersch, and Judith Wittner, "Becoming Social: School Girls and Their Culture Between the Two World Wars," *The Journal of Early Adolescence* 5 (Winter 1985): 479–88.

54. See illustrations in text. On the historical origins of romantic love, see Ira L. Reiss, *Premarital Sexual Standards in America* (New York: Free Press, 1960), pp. 53–59; Ellen K. Rothman, *Hands and Hearts: A History of Courtship in America* (New York: Basic Books, 1984), pp. 103–10; Nava, "Youth Service Provision . . . ," p. 15.

55. Jane Gallop, "Annie Leclerc Writing a Letter, with Vermeer," *October* 33 (Summer 1985): 103–18; Umberto Eco, "How Culture Conditions the Colours We See," in *On Signs*, ed. Marshall Blonsky (Baltimore: Johns Hopkins University Press, 1985), pp. 157–75; "Pink and Black Chosen for Show Theme," *Courier-Express*, Oct. 8, 1955, p. 11; issues of *Better Homes & Gardens*, 1952, 1954, 1955; Virginia Kelley interview, Oct. 20, 1985. Also Sonny Fisher,

recording, "Pink and Black Slacks." On the incorporation of mid-1970s "punk" subculture into the fashion mainstream, see Hebdige, *Subculture*, pp. 92–99.

56. Roll interview.

57. Rose Gallivan interview, Feb. 3, 1986; Petrelli interview; Roll interview.

58. Guarino interview (quotation); Petrelli interview; Roll interview.

59. Betty Lou Eisenmann interview, Dec. 10, 1985; Prince interview; Petrelli interview; Whitman interview. On the relationship between delinquency and frequency of attendance at a "hangout," see Edmund W. Vaz, "Juvenile Delinquency in the Middle-Class Youth Culture," in his *Middle-Class Juvenile Delinquency*, p. 144. On television, Jules Tygiel, review of Benjamin Rader's *In Its Own Image*, in *Reviews in American History* 13 (Dec. 1985): 623.

60. Kenneth T. Jackson, *Crabgrass Frontier: The Suburbanization of the United States* (New York: Oxford University Press, 1985), pp. 190–218. A similar white/black population shift occurred in Philadelphia; see John F. Bauman, *Public Housing, Race, and Renewal: Urban Planning in Philadelphia, 1920–1974* (Philadelphia: Temple University Press, 1987), pp. 58, 79, 83–87, 117, 149–51, 161–62. On Boston, see Mel King, *Chain of Change: Struggles for Black Community Development* (Boston: South End Press, 1981), pp. 7, 19–25. Phil Cohen describes the impact of high-rise housing on youth in London's East End in "Subcultural Conflict and Working-Class Community," excerpted in Hall and others, *Culture, Media, Language*, pp. 78–87. The gangs that arose to contest territoriality illustrate Cohen's conclusion that subcul-

tures represent an attempt to express and resolve "contradictions" within the parent culture (in this case, contradictions expressed as parental decisions to relocate). See the discussion of Cohen in Hall and Jefferson, *Resistance Through Rituals*, pp. 30–32. According to Bauman, "Much of the interracial conflict in [Philadelphia in] the 1950s involved teenagers" (*Public Housing*, p. 161).

61. Roll interview; Petrelli interview; *Courier-Express*, May 15, 1958, pp. 1–2.

62. Martin interview; Buffalo, Board of Education, *Minutes*, Nov. 12, 1953, p. 877; May 26, 1954, pp. 1303, 1310–11; Bihl interview.

63. The following material on juvenile delinquency and Dress Right is adapted from Graebner, "The 'Containment' of Juvenile Delinquency." On women's roles, see Susan M. Hartmann, *The Home Front and Beyond: American Women in the 1940s* (Boston: Twayne, 1982), p. 82 (quotation); and Andrea A. Walsh, *Women's Film and Female Experience, 1940–1950* (New York: Praeger, 1984), p. 75.

64. *Amherst Bee*, May 23, 1957; *Courier-Express*, "YMCA's Junior Leaders Answer Critics of Youth," May 19, 1957, both in YMCA clipping collection, "YMCA Scrapbook, 1957."

65. "Suspect in Attacks on 12 Riverside Girls Is Finally Committed," *Buffalo Evening News*, May 24, 1952, clipping in *Buffalo Evening News* files, "Wylegala"; *Courier-Express* cartoons on juvenile delinquency, Buffalo and Erie County Historical Society, Buffalo. On the paranoid climate of the late 1940s and early 1950s, see Edgar Z. Friedenberg, *The Vanishing Adolescent* (1959; New York: Dell,

1962), p. 176; George Chauncey, Jr., "The National Panic Over 'Sex Crimes' and the Construction of Cold War Sexual Ideology, 1947–1953," unpublished paper; and Estelle B. Freedman, "'Uncontrolled Desires': The Response to the Sexual Psychopath, 1920–1960," *Journal of American History* 74 (June 1987): 83–106.

66. New York State Youth Commission, *Program for Youth*, 1957, p. 29; Buffalo Youth Board, *Report*, 1957, pp. 25, 28. On games of "chicken," see "Teen Gang Rites Shock Probers of Hoodlumism," *Courier-Express*, June 15, 1955, p. 1; *Courier-Express*, July 9, 1955, pp. 1–2. On car theft as a middle-class youth crime, see William W. Wattenberg and James Balistrieri, "Automobile Theft: A 'Favored Group' Delinquency," *The American Journal of Sociology* 57 (May 1952): 575–79. According to anthropologist Barbara Myerhoff, mutilation, tattooing, and other adolescent rites of initiation are "often strikingly painful," forms of "culturally induced suffering that dramatizes what might otherwise be a mundane physiological change" ("Rites of Passage: Process and Paradox," in *Celebration: Studies in Festivity and Ritual*, ed. Victor Turner [Washington, D.C.: Smithsonian Institution Press, 1982], p. 121).

67. Undated clipping, Danny McBride Scrapbook; "Five Youths Agree to End Corner Idling," *Courier-Express*, Sept. 1, 1953, p. 11; "Foster Father Wins Leniency for Loungers," *Courier-Express*, Oct. 15, 1953, p. 28-A; "Judge Starts War on Teenage Gangs; 'Lounger' Is Fined," *Courier-Express*, Aug. 30, 1953, sec. B, p. 1; "Judge Frees Youths After Stern Talk," *Courier-Express*, Nov. 15, 1953, p. 21–B. See also Roland J. Chilton, "Middle-Class

Delinquency and Specific Offense Analysis," and Albert K. Cohen, "Middle-Class Delinquency and the Social Structure," both in Vaz, *Middle-Class Juvenile Delinquency*, pp. 96, 204, and 206, respectively.

68. Statement by Vincent Masterson, *The Herald*, Nov. 3, 1955; two *Courier-Express* clippings in Buffalo Boys Club scrapbook: "What Do You Think Causes Vandalism," March 30, 1954, and "Youth Leader Asserts City Needs 12 More Boys' Clubs," March 31, 1946; "Teen-Age Group Works for Community's Good," *Courier-Express*, Jan. 6, 1960, YMCA clipping collection (untitled volume of clippings from 1959–60); *Courier-Express*, Dec. 18, 1953, p. 6. On the content of street-corner lounging, see Paul Corrigan, "Doing Nothing," in Hall and Jefferson, *Resistance Through Rituals*, pp. 103–5.

69. Buffalo and Erie County, Council of Social Agencies, Survey of Recreational Needs, pp. 9, 10; clipping, editorial, from *Cold Spring Advertiser*, Sept. 23, 1954, in Buffalo Boys Club scrapbook; New York State Youth Commission, *Program for Youth*, p. 31; clipping, "Masten Boys Club Program Varied: It Keeps Them Busy and Off Streets," *Buffalo Evening News*, March 31, 1954, in Buffalo Boys Club scrapbook. Clipping, "YMCA Canteen Leaders Plan Own Program," *Courier-Express*, Jan. 3, 1957, in YMCA clipping collection, volume "YMCA Scrapbook, 1957"; clipping, "Teen Center Gets Wide Support," *Orchard Park Herald-Press*, July 7, 1960, in YMCA clipping collection, volume 1959–60; photo, *Courier-Express*, Dec. 29, 1957, in YMCA clipping collection, volume "YMCA Scrapbook, 1957"; clipping, "Teen Center to Open Oct. 1,"

Cheektowaga Times, Sept. 19, 1957, p. 1, in YMCA clipping collection, volume "YMCA scrapbook, 1957"; New York State Youth Commission, "Making Teen Centers Succeed," prepared by Sidney G. Lutzin (Albany, New York, 1953), p. 3; "Teen-Agers Club Helps Make Friends," *Courier-Express*, Oct. 13, 1955, p. 31.

70. *Buffalo Criterion*, Apr. 16, 1949, p. 3; May 12, 1951, p. 2 (editorial); and "Cold Springs Men on the Alert," Aug. 16, 1947, p. 7 (editorial).

71. "Fighting Priest Helps Round Up Hoodlums, Then Lectures Them," *Buffalo Evening News*, March 29, 1957, clipping in BEN files, "Working Boys Home"; Buffalo, Common Council, *Proceedings*, Jan. 1, 1957–Dec. 31, 1957, p. 1740; Warner Hessler, "Red Devil in a Roman Collar," *Courier-Express Sunday Magazine*, May 19, 1974, p. 4.

72. "CYC Group 'Takes Over' Reins of City," *Courier-Express*, May 10, 1953, p. 40-B; "Catholic Youth Activities," *Union and Echo*, Jan. 14, 1949, p. 8; "Youth Leaders to Attend Sessions," Oct. 2, 1949, p. 5; "Youth Convention February 6, 7, 8," Jan. 18, 1953, p. 10; "Several Parishes Have Own Papers," Apr. 17, 1955, p. 2; "Leaders Told to Let Youths Run Activities," *Courier-Express*, Sept. 29, 1953, p. 6.

73. Jim Lee interview by Mia Boynton, Nov. 19, 1985; column, "Catholic Youth," *Union and Echo*, Jan. 7, 1949, p. 12.

74. From *Union and Echo*: "Lack of Religion Aids Delinquency," Dec. 27, 1953, p. 10 (last quote); "Approve of Petting? Why," Oct. 16, 1955, p. 2 (first quote); "Going Steady," Oct. 18, 1953, p. 2 (middle quote); "Object to Sex Films," Apr. 17,

1949, p. 13; "Plan Marriage Course in Lent," Feb. 25, 1949, p. 5; see also "Verein Deplores Saturday Parties," Aug. 2, 1953, p. 2.

75. From *Union and Echo*: ratings, March 20, 1949, p. 5, and March 6, 1955, p. 5; "Legion of Decency" column, May 29, 1955, p. 12, and July 3, 1955, p. 5; see also "Youths Pick 'Cinerama,'" Dec. 18, 1955, p. 5. "All-Out War on 'Smut' Dealers Urged," *Courier-Express*, Oct. 4, 1955, p. 30.

76. The link between dress and behavior was a staple of 1950s social thought; see Ryan, *Clothing*, p. 295. The material on Dress Right is adapted from Graebner, "The 'Containment' of Juvenile Delinquency."

77. *Vocational Education, Buffalo—1937* (N.p., n.d.), p. 8. The search for homogeneity through the comprehensive high school is treated in James Bryant Conant, *Education in a Divided World: The Function of the Public Schools in Our Unique Society* (Cambridge, Mass.: Harvard University Press, 1948), and Nasaw, *Schooled to Order*, pp. 156–58. The Buffalo system of separate academic and vocational high schools came under heavy criticism from the New York State Department of Education; see New York State, State Education Department, *Buffalo Public Schools in the Mid-Twentieth Century: A Report of a Survey of the Public Schools of the City of Buffalo* (Albany: University of the State of New York, 1951), pp. 93–94, 114, 126, 131.

78. The progress of integration can be traced by counting faces in the school yearbooks. On integration at East High in 1953–54, see East High *Eastonian*, 1954 (N.p., n.d.), pp. 9, 14. On race relations in the 1940s, see Mark Goldman, "The Buffalo Desegregation Case," *Buffalo Spree*, Spring 1985, p. 48ff.

79. Girls Vocational High School, *The Herald*, 1947 (Buffalo, n.d.), p. 65; Fosdick-Masten Vocational High School, *The Herald*, 1958 (Buffalo, n.d.), p. 3. On the "hidden curriculum" in English girls' schools, see Brake, *Sociology of Youth Culture*, p. 140. Also see illustration in text.

80. Riverside High School, *Skipper*, 1946, unpaginated; Hutchinson-Central High School, *Calendar*, 1949, pp. 8–9; Bennett High School, *Beacon*, commencement issue, 1947, pp. 68–71; Riverside *Skipper*, 1947, p. 67. Separation during eating may be related to the association of eating with sex; see Edward A. Ross, *Social Control: A Survey of the Foundations of Order* (1901; reprint, New York: Macmillan, 1928), pp. 326, 331; William Graham Sumner, *Folkways: A Study of the Sociological Importance of Usages, Manners, Customs, Mores, and Morals* (New York: Ginn, 1906), pp. 458–59, 497, 409; and Sigmund Freud, *The Basic Writings of Sigmund Freud*, trans. and ed. A. A. Brill (New York: The Modern Library/Random House, 1938), pp. 586, 603.

81. Riverside *Skipper*, 1955, p. 33. Anthropologists seem to agree that modern American culture lacks significant puberty rites; see Turner, "Introduction," p. 25, and Myerhoff, "Rites of Passage," p. 130, in Turner, *Celebration*.

82. The material on maturity is adapted from William Graebner, "Coming of Age in Buffalo: The Ideology of Maturity in Postwar America," *Radical History Review* 34 (Jan. 1986): 53–74.

83. On dances in relationship to social

class, see A. B. Hollingshead, *Elmtown's Youth: The Impact of Social Classes on Adolescents* (John Wiley & Sons, 1949), pp. 302–7. On the prom, see Joseph W. Scott and Edmund W. Vaz, "A Perspective on Middle-Class Delinquency," in Vaz, *Middle-Class Juvenile Delinquency*, p. 220. Quotation from Bishop Timon High School, *The Talisman*, 1957, p. 70.

84. Nasaw, *Schooled to Order*, pp. 157–58; Joel Spring, *The Sorting Machine: National Educational Policy Since 1945* (New York: David McKay, 1976), pp. 44–49; Conant, *Education in a Divided World*, pp. 59–65, 72, 87, 109.

85. Holdsworth interview; Buffalo, Board of Education, *Minutes*, Jan. 24, 1951, p. 6755.

86. Fosdick-Masten Park, *The Chronicle*, 1947, p. 5 (quotation); also East High *Eastonian*, 1954, p. 11; Hutchinson-Central *Calendar*, 1953, pp. 14–17, and 1948, pp. 42–45; Riverside *Skipper*, 1949, p. 38; Bennett *Beacon*, commencement issue, 1948, p. 6.

87. Buffalo Technical High School, *Techtonian*, 1947, p. 9; Bennett *Beacon*, commencement issue, 1948, p. 6; Riverside *Skipper*, 1951, p. 48.

88. James S. Coleman, "Athletics in High School," *The Annals of the American Academy of Political and Social Science* 338 (Nov. 1961): 33–43, 52. Athletics were also a primary vehicle for the partial integration of black students and served to rationalize the class structure, as athletes learned that "we do the best we can regardless of how large or how small the job or problem is that confronts us along our way" (Riverside *Skipper*, 1950, p. 66). See also Willis Rudy, *Schools in the Age of Mass Culture* (Englewood Cliffs, N.J.: Prentice-Hall, 1965), and Joel Spring, "Mass Culture and School Sports," *History of Education Quarterly* (Winter 1974). On debate, see the following yearbooks: Buffalo Technical *Techtonian*, 1958, p. 68; 1946, p. 71; 1950, p. 54; 1955, p. 65; Grover Cleveland High School, *Clevelander*, 1958, p. 47; 1955, pp. 44–45; 1947, p. 46; Riverside *Skipper*, 1959, p. 86; 1957, p. 80; 1953, no page number; 1952, p. 66; 1948, p. 59. Quotation in Seneca *Chieftain*, 1951, "Yearbook Preface."

89. Seneca *Chieftain*, 1958, pp. 100–7; 1955, p. 10; Buffalo Seminary, *Seminaria, 1851–1951*, p. 15; 1953, p. 44; 1954, pp. 55–56; 1957, pp. 45–46; Riverside *Skipper*, 1945, no page number; 1947, p. 57. See Friedenberg's indictment of pseudo-democratic student government in *Vanishing Adolescent*, pp. 94–95.

90. East High *Eastonian*, 1954, pp. 46–47, 85, 50–51, 11, 14–15.

91. Lee interview by Boynton. "Checking the Dope Problem," *Buffalo Criterion*, Nov. 25, 1950, p. 2 (editorial); "Dope Peddlers," *Buffalo Criterion*, Feb. 2, 1952, p. 1.

92. Roll interview; Audrey Hackett interview, Sept. 26, 1985; William Robinson and Zaid Islam interview, Nov. 9, 1985; George J. Kunz, "Thrills, Chills and Cinnamon Suckers: A Crystal Beach Memory," *Buffalo Evening News Magazine*, Aug. 17, 1980, pp. 4–6; Mike Vogel, "Diamond Jim and His *Canadiana*," *Buffalo Evening News Magazine*, Aug. 17, 1980, pp. 5, 10; *Union and Echo*, June 12, 1949, p. 6. See also Wiebe, *Segmented Society*, p. 174.

93. James Pickens interview, Nov. 22, 1985; *Courier-Express*, May 31, 1956, p. 1;

Robinson and Islam interview.

94. The author obtained the FBI file on the *Canadiana* disturbance (File no. 45-9285) through a Freedom of Information Act request (no. 263,062); Margaret Wynn and Dick Hirsch, "Terror Marks Boatride," *Buffalo Courier-Express*, May 31, 1956, p. 1; Ed Gralnik interview, May 4, 1986.

95. Wynn and Hirsch, "Terror"; Pickens interview.

96. *Buffalo Evening News*, June 26, 1956, p. 1; "Deplore Black Conduct," *Buffalo Criterion*, June 2, 1956, p. 1; *Buffalo Evening News*, June 1, 1956, editorial, and pp. 1, 8; June 5, 1956, p. 26, editorial; June 2, 1956, p. 3.

97. Glaser interview; *Buffalo Evening News*, Dec. 8, 1956, pp. 1, 3; "Three Hurt in Gang Attacks; Police Round Up Suspects," *Buffalo Evening News*, Nov. 20, 1957, p. 57; *Courier-Express*, July 26, 1957, pp. 1, 3; May 15, 1958, pp. 1–2. On the Center Theater incident, see *Courier-Express*, Dec. 16, pp. 1, 3, and Dec. 17, 1957, p. 19; *Buffalo Evening News*, Dec. 16, 1957, pp. 1, 22; Daniel Majchrzak interview, July 19, 1983; Robert Rush interview, July 11, 1983. See also "Another Northern City Runs into Race Problem," *U.S. News & World Report*,

Apr. 18, 1958, pp. 90, 91, 93; Buffalo, Board of Community Relations, "Civic Unity," *Report*, July 1, 1956–June 30, 1957, p. 19.

98. In order to appreciate how the trouble on the *Canadiana* could have had such an impact, it might be helpful to see the incident as an example of the anthropology of celebration. Memorial Day on the *Canadiana* was an occasion of festive ceremony, at once a rite of spring and an affirmation of shared values. As a celebration, the occasion reconciled differences and held conflict in abeyance. That is, until 1956, when youths aboard the vessel engaged in what Victor Turner has called a "social drama," an "eruption from the level surface of ongoing social life" in which man "reveals himself to himself, . . . latent conflicts become manifest, [and] kinship ties . . . emerge into key importance." See Turner, "Introduction," in his *Celebration*, pp. 12, 16, 20; and his *The Anthropology of Performance* (New York: PAJ Publications, 1986), pp. 74–76, 81, 90, 92.

99. Peter Biskind, *Seeing Is Believing: How Hollywood Taught Us to Stop Worrying and Love the Fifties* (New York: Pantheon Books, 1983), pp. 202–5.

I N D E X